Home Country

Home Country

Richard Mabey

CENTURY
London Sydney Auckland Johannesburg

To Richard Simon

First published in 1990 by Random Century Group,
Random Century House,
20 Vauxhall Bridge Road, London SW1V 2SA

Random Century Australia (Pty) Ltd,
20 Alfred Street, Milsons Point, Sydney,
New South Wales 2061, Australia

Random Century New Zealand Limited,
PO Box 40-086, Glenfield, Auckland 10, New Zealand

Random Century South Africa (Pty) Ltd,
PO Box 337, Bergvlei, 2012 South Africa

Typeset in Imprint and Bernhard
by SX Composing Ltd, Rayleigh, Essex
Printed and bound in Great Britain
by Butler and Tanner Ltd, Frome, Somerset

British Library Cataloguing in Publication Data
Mabey, Richard, *1941-*
    Home country.
    1. Great Britain. Landscape
    I. Title
    719.0941

ISBN 0-7126-3720-6

Contents

Part One:

Making Tracks

I was about fifteen when I was first smitten by a landscape. It was an intense affair, with all the obsessiveness and muddling emotions of a teenage crush. I mooned around in it, tried to understand it, dreamed about it at nights.

Yet it was an ordinary enough patch, the landscape next door almost. It lay at the top of our road, centred on an old ridgeway track that meandered through a cluster of woods and commons. Below it was a shallow valley that wound away south into the Chilterns and which once in a while carried a thin stream, a winterbourne. Local legend had it as a woe-water that only flowed in times of trouble, and it had the unsavoury name of the Bourne Gutter. But I thought it was the most achingly beautiful view I had ever seen. There was one spot where I would stand on the track and gaze over the valley in something close to rapture. It was an unsettling feeling, numinous, indefinable, a sense of something just beyond reach. At times it turned into an actual physical sensation that made the back of my legs tighten, as if I was peering down from a great height. Perhaps it was just growing pains, or those intimations of spirituality that often strike adolescents.

The intensity of those feelings faded, thankfully, but my attachment to the place didn't, and for long stretches of my life the land between ridgeway and winterbourne served as a reference point where I went to get my bearings, escape, ponder, unwind, banish fits of the sulks. I learned about birds here, fell in (and out) of love, and have found that the scene repeatedly works its way into my writing. It has been through a whole generation of farming changes since I first knew it. Many of the hedges have gone, and a cluster of the woods. One wood, where I had unearthed tiny fragments of a crashed French fighter when I was a boy, vanished almost overnight in the late sixties. When I went back there one spring all that remained were the bluebell shoots obstinately pushing through the young wheat. A while later the whole valley was bought by an insurance company, and that summer the shooting was so intense that for the first time in my life I could not bear to go there. In a few years'

3

time, in a backhanded compliment to the Iron Age people who first tramped out the track, a four-lane bypass will sweep through the valley, dogging its route all the way.

The valley's spell, surprisingly, still survives 30 years on. I am up here again today, not entirely sure whether I'm trying to escape from writing or hoping to find something to write about. It is a mid-August heatwave, a halcyon day. The air is so clear that I can see the windows of Hemel Hempstead's office blocks flashing in the sun at the far end of the valley. It is hot enough for shorts, and I have walked up here across the harvest fields, with the sharp ends of the stubble digging into my legs – one of those delicious seasonal discomforts, like the feel of tar bubbles bursting on bare feet. Speckled wood butterflies are flickering in the gaps blown out of beeches by the gales, sketching out next year's regrowth. Down in a field below me a boy is sitting with his dog on top of a huge straw bale, the first solitary young person I have seen here since I was a teenager myself. It is a healing, generous kind of day, and I find phrases forming in my mind: 'how peaceful'; 'just like it used to be . . .'

Except that the valley, bone dry after the long summer, is full of herons. They are skulking in trees and picking their way through what is left of the grass. I watch one through binoculars as it changes one sullen roost for another. It flies up heavily to the top of an ash tree, crumples like a parachute, then shifts its weight on to one leg and freezes. The other birds are scattered about the meadows in similar poses – necks craned forward, waiting. They look awkward and misplaced, fish-eaters out of water.

Suddenly they are up and flying together, like a tattered sail over the stubble. I can count them now (there are eleven) and see the black heads of immature birds. Perhaps they are from one nesting colony and out hunting beetles. But such details seem pedantic beside the image of these loping marshland birds, English storks, beating over ground which has been baked ochre by the drought. For a moment it seems like a scene from the Middle East. Then I remember the last time I saw herons here, when the winterbourne was flowing and the valley was under water. It had been late March, a few years before. There were snipe and the first willow warblers about, and the floodwater had made sense of the whole geography of the valley, the sites of the few farms and boundary trees, and of the two herons that stood motionless at the very edge of the flood. The winterbourne itself had been like an upland burn, rushing over the meadow grass, making oxbows and lakes in the middle of flat fields, a real *spring*, and as far from a sign of woe as you could imagine.

It is never 'just like it used to be' here, or in any other halfway natural place I have seen. If there is one feature that marks out the countryside from other kinds of place it is that it grows, that its whole structure is in a state of continuous succession, death and rebirth. The natural world survives by renewal and serendipity and an inborn tenacity, and this is what has made it such a constant source of inspiration. It reminds us of our own physicality, of sharper and simpler vitalities. The bluebells force up through the wheat; the winterbourne rises like a sap; birds and butterflies become dowsers, sensing pasts and futures that we have become dull to.

I suppose it was this part pagan, part romantic conviction that was surfacing along the ridgeway when I was a teenager. Yet it was echoed in different ways as I got to know other landscapes. Each new place forced me to come to grips with a different aspect of our relationship with nature. Running wild in north Norfolk in my late teens and twenties I began to understand the idea of 'the edge', of where it lay between humans and nature, if at all, and that there was no such thing in nature itself – just a frayed margin, of opportunity and possibilities. Following the tracks of the eighteenth-century Hampshire naturalist, Gilbert White, I learned something of the subtle ways that the past persists in the natural world, not as a fossil but a living thread of continuity. And, coming at last to look after a patch of my own, an ancient wood in the Chilterns, I had to confront, at first-hand, the questions of where human responsibilities towards nature lie.

*

This book is an attempt to tell the story of how an attitude to nature was formed out of the experience of different landscapes. It is not quite an autobiography, but a collection of personal sketches of love affairs, in which landscapes rather than people are the principle characters (sometimes, alas, this was literally true).

The affairs have not always been tidy, or easy. I found out at an early age that a romantic relationship with the land, in which nature was regarded as a more or less equal partner with its own life to lead, was not the way one was supposed to regard it. No one ever spoke to me in quite the disdainful terms that Richard Jefferies' father used about his son ('our Dick poking about in them hedges') but it was made clear that the *correct* view of nature was decidedly not from the hedge looking out. The countryside had, of course, to contrast with the supposed pace and artificiality of the city, but not by becoming a refuge for freedom and spontaneity. It must rather be the place where landscapes (still man-made) are calm, 'timeless' and deferential, where nature becomes another kind of property.

This belief still persists in backwaters of the English countryside, but thankfully the larger idea that we have a divine right – or, worse, *duty* – to dominate nature is beginning to fade, and is being replaced with the concept of 'stewardship', where humans are seen as the good shepherds of the earth. It is a step forward in acknowledging that our real role on the planet is to be both part of nature, and, in some crucial ways, above it. Yet there are worrying signs that the new stewardship is going beyond honest protection towards haughty meddling, and is continuing, under a new label, the old crusade of re-making nature in man's image. The philosophy of stewardship has now reached the edges of Amazonia and Antarctica, where it is being argued that only by bringing the wilderness into commercial exploitation can it be saved. It is hard to know whether this is a policy of despair or the only realistic alternative to rampant destruction. But at times it looks as if it is just an attempt to complete the process started so disastrously by the Europeans in the seventeenth century.

Back home, the story seems much the same. On the few occasions in the last few years when it looked as if our iron grip on nature might be loosening a little (the release of surplus arable land and the hurricanes), the prospect seems to have unleashed a dormant nightmare, like a vision from a Dark Ages bestiary: the land turning into an impenetrable tangle of swamp and scrub, hiding plagues of vermin and in some unexplained way forfeiting for ever its hope of being 'green and pleasant'.

Increasingly, instead of being looked to as an alternative order, nature is being drawn into (and regarded as only viable within) the structure and discourse of the market place. Wild creatures are given protection only when they become scarce, not for their own sakes. Land, to be valued, must be productive, efficient, useful. If not, at least it must be Outstandingly Beautiful or of Special Scientific Interest. Ordinary common or garden land, relaxed land, land simply working out its own destiny, is called contemptuously *waste* land, and can only be redeemed by being pressed into service.

The vocabulary of those who run the land (or *manage* it) gives ominous hints about how they view it. Old woodland, for instance, is described as 'derelict', 'over-mature', 'senile', 'going to scrub', as if trees, the most successful and durable of plants, were incapable of living correctly without supervision. We still use that jarring, prelapsarian word 'reclamation' for the civilizing of wild places, as if we were grabbing back something we had literally once owned.

*

Perhaps this is part of the kind of species we are. I know I am not immune myself. Writing, my livelihood, is also my way of 'managing' nature, or making sense of it for my own purposes. It has even come to feel like a kind of land work, dependent on weather and the seasons and a fair helping of serendipity, and producing, with luck, a crop of so many words per acre tramped. The difference is that, for a writer, there is no such thing as poor soil. Almost anything – drought, pollution, hurricane, even a vision of sterility – can be harvested as productive copy. The gap between imagination and necessity is one that I still do not know how to close. Yet, as Fraser Harrison has written, our visions of nature may be part of its human importance: 'this is how the light could fade, not eclipsed by . . . the fog of pollution but put out by the blinding of our imagination.'

These days I spend more time at the far end of the track, where the country is wilder and still has breathing spaces. Along these wooded western reaches it is a kind of no-man's-land, undefined, poised between town and farming countryside, where the frontiers are still being contested. Follies and entrepreneurial schemes – for rock concerts, hotels, clay pigeon ranges, nature reserves – swarm around the edges of the planned bypass. The first land has already started to come out of farming, too. Near the source of the winterbourne a stretch of pasture has been given over to Christmas trees, but they are growing slowly and being remorselessly invaded by hazel and dogwood and field flowers from the hedgebanks. A couple of miles to the west a ragged ancient copse, Hardings Wood, fell out of the commercial forestry system, and, not entirely sure what I was doing, I bought it. I have tried to turn it into a community wood, run by and for the benefit of the parish, yet in one corner of my mind it is also a kind of private library, a huge resource for writing.

Who and what is the countryside for? Different images and claims have repeatedly collided, despite the myth of cosy rural unity. A few hundred yards from Hardings Wood, on the edge of the Tring Park estate where local commoners fought off a seventeenth-century enclosure, I found this message spray-painted on the back of a barn: 'If these hedges burn so will this barn.' The country around here is full of barricades and boundaries going back to the Celts. The latest embattlements line the commons and verges along the ridgeway itself. They were raised in the last few years to keep out the caravans of local gipsies and travellers, who in my childhood were liked and welcomed as long-established Chiltern citizens. In a century or two, weathered and their miserly purpose forgotten, perhaps they will join the ranks of local heritage sites.

William Hazlitt, trying to explain the roots of our love of the countryside, suggested that nature's renewal and familiarity made it 'a kind of universal home'. It would be nice to think this was true, and much of the time this is how it feels to me. Yet 'universal' is a difficult word for us to attach to home. Home is either our's or someone else's, and we have a long struggle ahead learning to accept that in our life with nature it has to be both.

Up by the ridgeway, of course, the herons are eternally hopeful and continue to dream like old prospectors of water deep under the ploughlines.

Home Ground

1

How does a child first perceive its own small spot of the earth? As a set of unrelated outside objects, or an already partially composed scene? Do unconscious needs for 'prospect and refuge' influence the ways we look at the world from the beginning or is a sense of place purely a matter of learning? I can't say how much adult editing has shaped – or at least fixed – my own first landscape memory, but I do know that it is also the earliest recollection of my life, and that it is a perfectly formed miniature pastoral, complete with background and meditating figure.

It is a fine summer morning in the middle of the Second World War. I am about two years old and toddling about the lawn gathering up the thin strips of silver paper which lie in the dew like gossamer. It fascinates me, this crop that springs up in the night, and I am vaguely aware that it falls out of the sky, from aeroplanes. But for the moment it is enough to have the damp and glistening bundles in my hand.

Forty years on I know it was called 'window' and that its purpose was to confuse enemy radar. But I am still mystified about who exactly scattered it and where, about how on earth it drifted as far as *our* garden, and why my sense of those early morning treasure hunts so overshadows the dim recollections of the rest of my early life.

I must also have gazed every day across the garden to the field of scratchy grass and frowsty ornamental trees that lay beyond it, and which was eventually to become a stepping stone out into the countryside beyond. But memories of that don't begin until I am about six. The images are detailed enough to have an aura of reliability about them – the layered branches of the Cedar of Lebanon after which our road was named, the wispy poplars along the borders, the three silver birches that rose like a classical trident on a mound directly aligned with our garden – and from which, as if to confirm its magical appearance, the first cuckoo always seemed to call. Beyond that, a vague sense of space and freedom hovers around the edge of the memories.

Or that is how I used to think it was. The truth has turned out to be slightly but unsettlingly different. I have a snap of this ancestral parkland which I took from an upstairs window in 1963. It is a wretched picture, already turning a livid chemical blue, and its terse, forensic labelling gives away the reason it was taken in such haste. This was to be a last record, before paradise was buried under a new estate.

Everything seems to be in the right place – our greenhouse, the laurel hedge, a prodigious spreading plane tree – but it all seems oddly distorted, too bunched up, too literal. And, embarrassingly clear on their mound are *two* birch trees, not quite the stuff out of which fantastic pagan groves are made.

Whatever else it may be, a child's map of the landscape is nothing like an adult's. It is less a matter of looking than touching and using. Or, perhaps, of marking. Perhaps we recapitulate historical relationships with landscape, just as individual human embryos repeat the fishy and amphibious evolution of the species. We grow up through (and maybe never entirely shed) a whole gamut of responses – an instinctive, animal sense of territory, a spell of animism, various Dark Age brews of magic and primitive science – before graduating to the sensible adult view of landscape as real estate.

*

My parents had come to this corner of the Chilterns a few years before the war. They were born and bred Londoners who'd met through their jobs in the City, and the move was, at the time, more a prudent side-step than a real retreat to the country. As part of his work as an accountant with one of the clearing banks my father had been on a fact-finding trip to Germany in 1936, to scout out new office technology. The party had toured some of the big business machine factories and their hosts had boasted about the flexibility of their plant. A slight shift in the diplomatic climate, a hint of war, and it could be converted to small arms manufacture in a trice. By a bleakly ironic coincidence my father's party were staying at the same hotel as a National Socialist convention with Hitler himself in blustering attendance. Within a short while, in no doubt about what lay ahead, my father and mother had made plans to move out of London.

I have no idea what made them choose the Chilterns – except that it was the first large stretch of countryside on what, from a German viewpoint, was the far side of London. Berkhamsted was then a small market town only an hour by train from Euston, and surrounded by woods and commons. It was already becoming popular as a commuter centre, and was on the edge of what the Metropolitan Railway Company had begun to popularize as 'Metroland' in the early thirties. The company's legendary advertising campaign somehow managed to combine an image of settled homeliness with an appeal to the frontier spirit: 'This is a good parcel of English soil in which to build home and strike root, inhabited from old, as witness the lines of camps on the hill tops and confused mounds amongst the woods, the great dyke which crossed it east and west, the British trackways, the Roman road aslant the eastern border, the packhorse ways worn deep into the hillsides, the innumerable fieldpaths which mark the labourers' daily route from hamlet to farm. The new settlement of Metroland proceeds apace, the new settlers thrive amain.'

No wonder prospective settlers queued up. Here, for the price of a small deposit, were instant ancestral roots, parts in an historical pageant whose origins could be traced back down ancient trackways as far as the Celtic twilight, and where work (at least by 'labourers') was still a sacrament not a chore. Ironically, making allowance for their deliberately antique phrasing, Metroland's blandishments were not a bad description of the Chiltern landscape. What is hard to see in them is any inkling of the dishevelled, hybrid patch of land on which my parents, fleeing from Norwood and the bombs to come, struck their new roots.

The house was built in 1935 as part of a large cluster of re-
spectable redbrick villas ('residences', the estate agents
called them, adding an instant sense of old habitation). The
land had once been part of the grounds of a Georgian mansion which had passed its last years as the home of Graham
Greene's uncle Charles and his large family. The Berkhamsted area had been thoroughly colonized by the
Greenes, who, as Graham was to write later, 'seemed to
move as a tribe like the Bantus, taking possession'. The
embryo novelist was a frequent visitor to the Hall and had a
secret eyrie on the roof, where he would gaze loftily over the
well-ordered meadows and shrubberies below, unaware
that they too would shortly become fertile playgrounds for
youthful imaginations: 'I would sit up there with my cousin
Tooter, consuming sweets bought with our weekly pocket
money . . . and discussing possible futures – as a midship-
man in the Navy or an Antarctic explorer – none of them to
be realized, while we watched the oblivious figures in the
yard and the stables from our godlike secrecy and security.'

To judge from the surviving photographs, the Hall was a
gloomy and graceless pile that cast a shadow over a considerable stretch of the High Street, and no one appears to
have mourned its demise. Its decline began just after the
First World War, when many big estates were broken up.
The western half of its grounds was sold off for a council
estate in the mid-twenties, and our commuters' houses
were added on the east side ten years later. The Hall itself
survived for a while as a boys' prep school, but became infested with dry rot and had to be razed to the ground.

That, though, wasn't quite the end of it. Its dismembered remains lingered on the site for decades, and gave the
new settlers of the Hall Park estate the chance to join in the
ancient rural custom of property recycling. Turves from
the tennis court were relaid as back-lawns, and handmade
bricks delicately pointed up for compost heap supports and
cold frames. My father, an inveterate magpie, managed to
find some elegant slabs of marble and laid them out as

shelves in his greenhouse, which gave it the odd air of a fish-and-chip shop.

*

The war my father had anticipated came, and London and south-east England were being raided almost nightly by the *Luftwaffe* during the year I was born. The bombers rarely ranged as far north-west as the Chilterns, but I don't have a single early memory which isn't in some way connected with the Blitz. Perhaps war, like sex, conveys to children some intuitive sense of its importance long before they realize what it is about. The memories are purely visual, like film clips or a series of tableaux, and more or less divorced from any emotions. Not far away city kids were rummaging for twisted shards of shrapnel in still smoking ruins. I gathered tinsel in the dew, a remote, uncomprehending spectator.

Not that there wasn't plenty to see. I loved to watch the languid sway of the local barrage balloons (though feeling I *was* one, vastly over-inflated, became a symptom of a nervously deranged digestion a few years later), and listen to the throb of Flying Fortresses taking off from the base at Bovingdon, on top of the next hill. By day there was the occasional distant dog-fight to watch, and in the evenings I would stand on a chair and peek out through the blacked-out windows at the lattice-work of searchlight beams in the sky. Early in the war a stray German bomb hit Sunnyside railway bridge a quarter of a mile away over the valley and blew a small chip out of Dad's pilfered greenhouse marble – a war-wound I prized for years. The air-raid sirens caused brief butterflies, but the closest I got to feelings of danger was gas-mask drill. I took a fearful thrill in the suffocating press of rubber on bare cheek, and the eerie strangled note it gave to your voice.

Only on two occasions did I have any inkling that some more deadly business was going on. I remember my father standing at the French windows in pyjamas, clinging to his

Home Guard rifle, and watching with quite contagious anxiety as an unidentified parachutist drifted down over the town. Then, towards the end of the war, being in my mother's bed during a rocket raid, hearing a buzz-bomb's motor stop directly overhead and feeling her arms tightening around me – a memory so vivid and physical it still makes me feel shaky to recall it.

The rocket drifted on towards Aylesbury I believe, and the realities of what was happening just 25 miles away seemed, to a child anyway, barely to cast a ripple across the fields. Land Army girls worked on the farms and Italian PoWs looked after the local woods. The remains of the Hall's grounds between the two new estates were grazed in a desultory way. By 1944, local damage from the renewed air raids was so slight that the Home Guard took to recording animal casualties: 'a fox was killed and a wood pigeon so badly injured it had to be destroyed'. The war, for me, ended as it had begun, as a series of distant vignettes, and reading accounts of the Home Front now I get a nagging feeling of guilt and longing that I glimpsed some of its outlines but knew nothing of either its horror or its conviviality. Even the dog-fighting spitfires seemed as comforting as swallows.

It had been a parochial experience, too, all observed from our house and garden at the edge of Berkhamsted. It was only at the end of the war that I began to go further afield – toddling off with my father to one of the village pubs beyond the town. We went the couple of miles to Bourne End along the canal towpath, where narrow boats carrying coal and china from the Midlands were still drawn by horses, or northwards to the common and Potten End, where the pub stood at the edge of a pond full of newts and tadpoles. This route took us up a deep lane called Bulbeggars, past pill-boxes and a row of concrete, pear-shaped 'tank-traps'. Already these wartime artefacts, like our ARP stirrup-pump and the pack of yellowing field-dressings kept in the bookcase with the Charles Dickens set, were beginning to look like curiosities, ripe for recycling. (The

concrete tank-traps have rather surprisingly survived, perhaps because of their sheer bulk, but have had to endure all
kinds of redefinition. They now block off a path across a
huge arable field just a few yards from their original site. A
little while ago I overheard two walkers earnestly discussing their ancient geological origins as erratics, swept here
by the last glaciers.)

But if I was beginning to see more of the parish, I had no
idea of local geography, or even, when it came to it, much
sense of direction. I would come home to the wrong front
door, wait for lifts in misidentified cars. On my very first
day at kindergarten I spent a half-hour of total misery trying to understand a lesson in fractions as a result of being
exactly in the middle of a room containing two classes back
to back, and not realizing I was facing the wrong way.

*

It was the site of that demolished mansion beyond our garden where the outside world began gradually to take shape.
We called it simply The Field, as if there wasn't another
worth bothering about. When our local gang began playing
there in earnest in the spectacular summer of 1948, it was
already going back to the wild, its exotic trees under siege
by a rising tide of hawthorn scrub and an irresistible aura of
scruffiness.

The Field was about a quarter of a mile square, and was
divided from our gardens by gappy rows of laurel and
poplar and occasional strands of barbed wire. It was owned
by the builder who had put up the new estate, an expatriate
Welshman called Gorwyn with a brooding Celtic counte-
nance. He had, I think, ancestral dreams of the pastoral
life, and occasionally put out a few Highland cattle to graze
or harrowed an acre or two of the rough grass. But he was
easy-going and fond of children and never seemed the least
put out that the entire neighbourhood used his field as their
local common. There was a track worn diagonally across it,
where commuters walking back from the station would

leave the main road and strike off home, along a short cut through the tussocks and cow-pats. Radiating from this track were less distinct paths that led to individual houses. Some ended in a homemade stile (ours was a pile of bricks from the bomb-shelter) and every evening at about six o'clock, a thin trickle of dark-suited men fanned out across the Field and picked their way over the barbed wire, out of the wilderness and into the vegetable patch.

But for us children who lived next to it, the Field wasn't just a waste-patch or short cut. It was a whole country, with a complex, aboriginal geography. It had its sacred sites and meeting places and initiation grounds. We may not have given much thought to how it looked, but we knew what every stone and bush was *for*. A considerable number, on reflection, seemed to be for hiding in. There was a sprawling hawthorn bush just ten yards from our fence that was my personal refuge; a labyrinthine holm oak, the best tree for climbing in the whole Field if you had the nerve; and beyond that, more thickets of yew and ivy shrouding the remains of the Hall walls. If you pushed and burrowed hard enough they all had spaces inside where the prickly mass of twigs and incurving branches seemed to have left a hollow, a calm centre. It was always exactly tailored to your own shape and size, and always seemed impregnable. I don't think I was an especially solitary child at that stage, or that there was anything at home that I needed to escape from. But the appeal of a personal lair, an invisible site in which to lie up, seemed precious even then.

But chiefly the Field was a sociable place, and its territory was marked out by the shared needs and conventions of our neighbourhood tribe. There were about ten of us who used to play there regularly, mostly middle-class children aged between seven and 11. There were two sets of brothers and sisters from higher up the hill; Ann, my tomboy best friend from across the road with whom I'd retired to a tent in the garden when I was five and planned an elopement; Tony, son of a high church banker and our clan elder, and Oscar, the teenager from the other side of the tracks, who taught us more than we should have known.

Despite its advance towards jungle, the Field was by no means a blank sheet historically. Its surface was strewn with evidence of its previous incarnation as the grounds of a big house. Gardens and terraces had grassed over into passable imitations of strip lynchets. Old flower-beds had become suburban tumuli. They seemed to retain some kind of aura, too (or perhaps just a topographical logic), because we often found ourselves unwittingly echoing their old functions.

The site of the well always seemed to have a quietening influence. We sat with our backs against the well-head and chatted and gazed as if we were by the side of a stream. The piles of rubble that were all that remained of the Hall's buildings had just the opposite effect. They were like long barrows – or forts – and tempted us into furious brick fights. I can still feel a chip of loose bone above one ear that was the result of one of these bloody encounters.

But our chief bases were on the level patches that had once been courtyards and terraces. This is where we built our camps and had solemn tribal meetings. The best was on what I suspect was once the Hall's tennis court. It had been scalloped into a steepish part of the hill, creating a plateau sheltered by steep banks on two sides. This was our gathering ground, and by sliding down to the bottom of one of the banks we could be certain of being invisible from our houses. We told dirty stories there and experimented with tentative gropings. It provided cover, too, for our shoddiest ritual, which was the capture – and mild torture, occasionally – of children from the estate on the other side of the Field, part of the then ceaseless war between Grammar Diggers and Council Bugs.

That was about as far as we went in the hunting side of the hunter-gatherer's life, and by and large we had a good relationship with the other creatures who lived in the Field. Gorwyn let us play with the Highland cattle when they took up temporary residence, though I suspect my faint memory of riding one is a fantasy. We collected butterfly chrysalises on their dried grass stalks to hatch out in jam jars, and stocked makeshift aquariums with newts and sticklebacks. We took birds' eggs too, following the rule about no more than one from each nest. But we wouldn't have dared pillage the nest of our resident barn owls, which were the Field's mascots, in a way. They lived in what had been the Greenes' stables, close to the High Street, and in the evenings hunted along a beat that almost exactly corresponded to our own territorial boundaries – up along the old garden wall of the Hall, past the abandoned orchard and back under the tall poplars. The sight of their soft feathers glowing burnished gold against the new spring leaves is one of the few purely visual memories of that time that have stayed perfectly vivid.

Depending on our moods and the seasons we moved nomadically round the Field, lighting fires, gathering flints, doing a little balsa-wood whittling or kite-flying or whatever was the latest craze. But we were never far from a tree. Trees were at the heart of our tribal culture. They were totems, landmarks, sources of raw materials. We did not know all their names, but knew which provided the best wood for building and which for burning, which smelt the worst, which were the most thrilling to climb. Sometimes we would spend whole mornings up the huge Cedar of Lebanon at the very top of the Field. Its lower levels were more like a barn than a tree, a cobwebbed labyrinth of aerial passageways full of choking dust from decades of trapped needles. Further down the hill was an ancient walnut, a prolific fruiter that we used to pelt with stones in the autumn to bring down the nuts. It was also a strategic tree, being next to the main track where it skirted the old tennis court. One day, with a show of precocious enterprise that still slightly shocks me, I set up a stall on an orange box here, right by the path. I had pillaged our vegetable garden for radishes and young carrots, and that evening hawked them to the homebound commuters.

Even fallen trees had their uses. When a big sweet chestnut blew down in a gale one night, I don't remember feeling anything other than breathless excitement at the awesome mass of it, and at the tangle of splintered wood and compressed foliage that had abruptly added an intriguing new dimension to the surface of the Field. We may have lost a nut harvest, but we had gained the novelty of horizontal tree-climbing and a spectacular new play space. There was a hole as big as a cave under the chestnut's torn-out roots, and down there, among the tangy scents of ginger and moss and wet clay, we built one of our longest-lived dens.

Most of our dens were in trees of some sort – usually tucked between their trunks or perched a few feet up in the lower branches. Building them was a job for the spring or early part of the summer holidays, and their style depended on what materials were at hand. We normally chose clumps of birch trees as our uprights, and used the easily-cut outer branches of poplar to make the framework for the roof and walls. We tied them on with gardener's twine, and covered them with switches of evergreen laurel, whose big, rubbery leaves were like a natural oilskin.

In fine weather we went out to these dens directly after breakfast and didn't come back until teatime. Sometimes, as we sat in the flickering shade surrounded by lashed branches and kitchen bric-à-brac borrowed from our mothers, they seemed to be transformed into magic rafts, which had freed us from the tethers of home and on which we could dream of being in other huts, in the Amazon jungle, or the South Seas of *Coral Island*.

We learned an odd mixture of cooking skills, too, part hardbitten backwoodsmanship, part old-fashioned cottage cuisine. We roasted potatoes in the ashes of our fires, made delicate concoctions out of soaked rose petals, chewed young hawthorn leaves straight off the bush, sucked honey out of phlox flowers and pounded almonds gathered from the front garden trees. One summer we worked out a way of making our own butter. We had an old tyreless bicycle, which we managed to turn into a kind of churn. We took off the mudguards, rested it upside down on its saddle, and strapped a small screw-top jar of cream to the rim of the back wheel. We took it in turns to hand-crank the wheel with the pedals, and about an hour later had a small, gelatinous, bland but totally gratifying knob of butter. Next time we remembered to add the salt.

I'm not sure where these ideas came from, or how, with the absolute minimum of debate, we agreed our rough-and-ready geography of the Field. No one presumed to be the clan leader, or to claim any special privileges beyond those that came anyway from superior age and strength. All our families were immigrants to the countryside, and none of us had access to any inherited rural lore. I think our Field-craft, such as it was, was simply cobbled together as we went along, out of ideas picked up from *Boys' Own Paper* adventure stories and a growing, intuitive familiarity with our native patch.

Many years later, when I became fascinated by maps and their history, I learned that in parts of the Caroline Islands in the Pacific, the inhabitants had plans of their home ground tattooed on their skins. That was what the Field felt like then, a second skin, prickly with sensations, taken for granted, full of meaning and association but never just an abstraction or symbol.

The instinctive assumption that a landscape was something you looked out *from*, not at, stuck, and I was well into my teens before I began to look at any part of the countryside as a 'view'. Sometimes a corner of the Field – or some other place I had got to know – would have a tree blown down or some undergrowth cleared. At first sight I was only ever aware of an uncomfortable sense that something was amiss. I needed to go in there and look back to realize what it was.

2

I doubt that our experiences in the Field were very different from those of most children growing up in the late forties and early fifties, before the free spaces in both town and country began to close up. But for me they represented the sum of my life beyond home and school. Except for the well-trodden routes I trailed down with my father, I had been nowhere. I hadn't any idea of the history of the place I lived in, and certainly no sense of the Chilterns as a geographical region. I don't think I even saw any difference between town and country, since each seemed to slip imperceptibly into the other here.

Prep school, just half a mile away in the town centre, was a partial help. One of our teachers, Mrs Benson, was a local naturalist, and she regularly took us out into the field for our nature periods. We would walk in crocodile formation up to a small wooded common on the plateau to the south of the school. Brickhill Green had once been the site of old brick-clay diggings, and had developed into a marvellous muddle of ponds, pits and scrub. In summer we dipped the ponds for newts and sticklebacks, watched whirligig beetles spinning madly about on the surface, and learned about the extraordinary air-filled diving bell which the water spider spins for itself, a miniature den in an underwater bubble. Later in the year Mrs Benson took us on fungus forays, and I can still taste the spicy freshness of those October walks and recall the sight of my first fly agaric toadstools in gold-tinged bracken under the birches.

In many schools 'nature study' was a notoriously soft subject, a cross between handicrafts and treasure hunting in which wild animals sometimes became indistinguishable from cuddly toys (though at least that was preferable to being regarded as laboratory specimens). We were lucky to have the best of both its aspects – the fun of squeezing purple plasticine into the shapes of toadstools, and some first real glimpses into what ecology was about.

By the time I was nine I had a keen interest in natural history, and a much tougher attitude towards it than I have now. I had one special moment of glory in Form 2 when the classroom decor was dominated for weeks by two of my biological trophies – a perfectly preserved dead bat and a large, explicit diagram of the male anatomy. I'd found the bat, a pipistrelle, impaled on a car radiator. It was still warm from the sun reflected off the chrome and seemed completely undamaged. I was rivetted by its look of composure and the silkiness of its wings, and stroked it distractedly all the way to school. Perhaps I thought I could coax it back to life. Mrs Benson put it in a jar filled with alcohol and stood it on a shelf at the back of the class.

The drawing was my earnest (or brazen) response to a homework project to draw a human body. I had a huge advantage over my classmates in possessing a textbook called *Anatomy and Physiology for Nurses*, which I'd persuaded my parents – how and why are an unplumbable mystery now – to buy me as a Christmas present. I'd meticulously copied one of its full-frontal diagrams on to the largest piece of paper I could find. To his credit our formmaster played fair with what was clearly homework beyond the call of duty, and stuck it up on the wall, fastidiously labelled patella, penis and all.

But when I moved down the hill to the 'Big School' at the age of 11, the world began to shrink again. Nature study was replaced by biology and confined to the laboratory with its perpetual stink of formalin and dismembered dogfish. Geography was more or less limited to what was still coloured red on the map. As for history, it was a discipline in all senses of the word, and the teaching staff were preoccupied with the forms and preservation of authority. Our syllabus could have been not unfairly summed up by history's own three Rs – Romans, Restoration, and Revolutions (Agrarian and Industrial). Our home parish would have been completely ignored but for the fact that it had two physical links with this authorized history. The High Street followed the route of a Roman Road to Verulamium (St Albans) and our ruined castle had connections with the Normans – one of the other civilizing agents highly regarded by our teachers. Just a few days before Christmas 1066, the Saxons ceded victory to William at Berkhamsted castle, next to what is now the railway station and turned him into the Conqueror – a dreadful smirch on the town's reputation.

But beyond that we learned little about the history of the town and its surrounding countryside; nothing of the common that pre-dated both Romans and Normans, and which was to become the scene of a great battle against nineteenth-century enclosure, and not much more about the coming of the canal and railway that had so profoundly changed the character of the whole area.

But a chart of the town did begin to form in my mind, coloured by habit and superstition just as the ground plan of the Field was – only in this one there were rather more sea-monsters than island refuges. The town was a mine-field, full of danger zones where one might be ambushed by rival gangs, bump into a master, or just stray into that mystifyingly irrational state of being 'out of bounds'. The canal was out of bounds in term-time. So – except for absolutely necessary journeys – was the High Street on Saturday mornings, full as it was with the lurid temptations of record shops and coffee bars and girls.

Being a day boy, and living half a mile from the school, my life was full of unavoidable journeys – back and forth to school twice daily, and up to games three times a week. The playing fields lay on top of the hill to the south of the town, right next to the ridgeway, and whichever route I took, cross-country along the track or up the road from the town centre, I had to pass perilously close to the local secondary modern school. Unless I was part of a group, I biked or walked in a state of more or less continuous alert, fearing that at any moment I would be jumped on, debagged, given Chinese burns, tied to a tree (or worse, inside a phone box) or any of the other horrors we dreamed of inflicting on *them*.

None of this ever happened, but we still crept about like timid bushmen, peering down alleys for strange faces, hiding up in old bomb shelters, dashing down short cuts, holding our collars for luck whenever we saw an ambulance, avoiding cracks between the paving stones at all costs, and relishing those moments of elation when we broke the rules or ran the gauntlet and got away with it.

But a good deal of this fear was self-induced or illusory, built on overheard conversations and half-understood local legend. On my cross-country route to games I passed through a stretch of parkland in which there was a group of wooded pits fenced off with iron railings. Somehow I had got hold of the idea – muddled maybe by stories about the eccentric, animal-collecting Rothschilds who had lived in the next town – that these had once been enclosures for exotic animals. I am fairly sure now that the fencing was to keep ordinary farm animals out from the workaday marl pits inside. But the belief wouldn't go away and, after long winter rains when the railings stood in seeping, viscous mud, I would hurry past, half afraid that some long-buried reptile was on the point of slithering free.

Even in the centre of the town there were fearful places. In the yard of the parish church a yew tree grew on a mound which reputedly housed the corpses of the town's plague victims. It lay by the corner of the road that joined the school with the High Street, and on the path of a natural short cut. But it needed just as much irreligious pluck to run over its roots as it did to dash through the rosemary bushes in the school's Garden of Remembrance, a place which lay under such a cloak of rules and sanctity that it seemed an even chance that entering would bring divine retribution as well as prefectorial.

Always, contrasting with our pinched, underground parish, there was this other territory of adult – or at least older boy – privilege: the grass quad, the cinemas, the railway station, and London, the other end of the line. There was also, closer to home, the Wilderness, a dingy cobbled lane between the school woodwork shop and the butchers, where we were convinced that one of the old cottages was a whorehouse offering special favours to school prefects.

It's remarkable that I didn't come to loathe this whole tract of land around the centre of the town, with its taboos and ancient feuds. But I was never really frightened – just kept in a state of edginess, of trying to keep ahead of the game and become what I suppose was a fifties equivalent of streetwise. And as a domain it had nothing of the deadly oppressiveness of the landscape to the north of the town, the wild tracts of the common where all manner of travails were devised to try and make men of us.

Berkhamsted's skyline is dominated by this vast expanse of bracken, scrub and beechwood. It stretches from one side of the parish boundary to the other and, together with the Ashridge woodlands with which it merges, covers close on six square miles. It was here long before the beginnings of the manorial system, though the Normans, who had the cheek to call it 'the foreign wood', snipped off a patch next to the castle for a deer park. In 1866 it was liberated from the grasping schemes of Lord Brownlow by a fantastic night raid by London navvies, hired by the townspeople. Since the twenties, when the old common rights had been extinguished and the commoners' sheep taken off, the heather had begun to revert to bracken, and birch and oak to colonize the open spaces. The descendants of the Normans' fallow deer relished the changes and expanded into a sizeable herd. They raided allotments and gardens on the north side of the valley but had never, so local lore claimed, crossed the road and railway to reach the woods on the south side. They were the common's familiar spirits, wild but territorially loyal. But at the time I knew nothing of this romantic history and was content with the Field, the common that, so to speak, lay on my doorstep.

Every road from the north side of the town ran through the common. The one we were obliged to follow most often climbed past the castle and Kitchener's Field, where an old woman tramp occasionally used to sleep – without any harassment – in a hollow tree lined with newspapers. It continued on through a cutting, across the path of the inscrutable earthwork known as Grim's Ditch, up to a memorial to the Inns of Court regiment which had trained on the common during the First World War.

It ought to have been a pleasant and interesting lane, except that, whenever the weather was too bad for rugby, we were despatched up it on a compulsory run that in its most sadistic version plunged into the wasteland just before the memorial, along a rutted path euphemistically called the Broad Track. Every drenching Tuesday and fogbound Thursday in winter I would toil through some combination of hill and mud, racked with stitch and ripped by brambles. And until my last couple of years at school the common was indelibly associated with pain, nausea and sodden clothes. It cast its blights quite indiscriminately, even on the school's cross-country team. Pritchard, a natural but mutinous athlete, renowned for begging illicit lifts and being able to smoke on the trot, used to return from the thickets with an exquisite sense of tragicomedy. He would fling himself through the finishing tape, collapse on the quad, and then go quietly off to retch up the dog-ends he had swallowed while dodging the marshals. Barnes, a blond and loping long-distance star idolized by the younger boys, once came back from a record-breaking run with his legs covered in vast weeping blisters. The school doctor said he had been scratched by an 'infected gorse bush'. And this the plant that local guidebooks called 'the glory of the common'! I had little doubt that the whole place was poisonous.

It came as no great surprise when I learned later that our distinguished ex-pupil Graham Greene – made utterly miserable by the isolations associated with being the headmaster's son – had made his first suicide attempt on the common when he was 13. Long before his undergraduate dabblings with Russian roulette, he would sneak up to hide among the gorse, and one day deliberately ate a bunch of deadly nightshade. I don't think he had written about this then, and we certainly hadn't read it. Greene was frowned on at school partly for his unsettling books, but chiefly, I suspect, because of the views he was known to hold about his time at Berkhamsted. This, of course, made him a hero among the boys, and Greene stories and myths rapidly found their way into playground gossip. We understood little of what lay behind his unhappiness or the kind of escape the *maquis* on the hill represented for him. To us, the suicide attempts were just brilliantly original stunts, two fingers stuck up at the school. They seemed on a par with a trick fashionable at school in those days in the mid-fifties, a ritual sequence of deep breathing and squatting that made one faint clean away on the classroom floor.

The town didn't share my distrust of the common. It was one of the few matters over which the entire population, right across the classes, was united. It seemed able to touch those romantic feelings for liberty and rights that were normally kept well below the surface in a property-owning community like Berkhamsted, and had been looked on as a local asset since before Norman times. But local people had only been granted any legal rights there comparatively recently. When the Brownlow estate was sold off to pay death duties in 1920, half of the common was bought as a gift for the National Trust, and the other half by the local golf club. A few years later the club granted the townspeople the right of 'air and exercise' over their holdings, under the provisions of the Metropolitan Commons Act.

The relationship has remained a slightly uneasy one. Local gleaners haunt the heather looking for golf balls which aren't always entirely lost. Non-golfers out for strolls brave the curses and stray balls of the foursomes and stride across the fairways. It isn't so much their legal rights they are asserting as a sense of the common as a shared inheritance, a sanctuary, a seam of 'good ground' standing watch over the town. I once heard the High Street butcher, one stiflingly hot day, explaining to a customer that he always kept the back door of the shop open to 'let in the fresh air from the common'.

Eventually the common got under my skin too, thanks to some more congenial school duties there. Because I had objections to joining the cadet corps I had ended up in the school scout troop, a stroke of good fortune for which I have been grateful ever since. It was a democratic and easy-going organization, without any obvious class or cultural barriers, and, in retrospect, rather Green, too. I learned cooking and map-reading and a sense of what I can only call environmental manners. Much of this has stayed with me, and even tying a clove-hitch in the dark hasn't turned out to be the fatuous activity it's usually mocked as. Once a term both scouts and corps decamped for a day of outdoor activities up on the common. The cadets played war-games; we had outdoor cooking competitions and orienteering exercises. The occasions were called – piquantly, for a few of us – Field Days, and, back messing about with trees and fires, I began to feel comfortable with the place at last.

Days in the Field itself had started to decline some years before. As we neared our teens the tribe began to break up. The older members were discovering sex in earnest, and days hidden in the lee of the old tennis court became more fervid and experimental. One day Ann, Tony and Oscar retreated into the den under the chestnut tree for some serious exploration, and ordered all us younger ones to stay outside. I felt muddled and excluded, and threw in a holly branch, which I felt would be useful, or necessary. But I remained blithely unaware of the crass symbolism of what I was doing. Some things in *Anatomy and Physiology for Nurses* were simply not to be believed.

We became sullenly competitive, too, challenging each other to painful endurance tests and tortures that had previously been reserved for the council boys. We gritted our teeth and walked barefoot across the flints and nettles, and saw how long we could endure a grass stalk twisted in the hair. One parched summer day we decided to set fire to the grass, just for the hell of it, and started a blaze that had us running panic-stricken to our parents. They kept a closer and more suspicious eye on us after that, and the romance of our communal refuge began to fade irretrievably.

*

The Field had one last, if marginal role, to play. It became a forecourt to the laboratory that my father let me start at the end of the garden. Actually laboratory is too grand a description. It was more of a glass-framed hut, an end bay of our greenhouse which had outlived its usefulness for forcing carnations. I suppose it was about six feet square, with shelves made out of concrete blocks. A young grape-vine strained against the back windows, and through the laurel hedge which overhung the front I could look straight out at the nearest of the Field's big hawthorn clumps.

I'd been a tinkerer with things vaguely scientific since I was about five, encouraged by the gadgets my father brought home from London. They were often stuffed into his briefcase with the bizarre bits of meat he picked up at Smithfield, and were a kind of technological offal them-selves: war-surplus weather kites, hand-cranked field dyna-mos, eye surgeons' scalpels, spools of wire, valves, the latest edition of *Practical Mechanics* . . . anything that might, as he always put it, 'come in useful one day'. It usually did, in that manic array of childhood busy-ness that still has me puzzling about how we crammed it all in.

Between building model planes and growing cacti I had worked my way through several electricity and chemistry sets (which in those days were magnificent wooden treasure chests of top grade glassware and chemicals), and had arrived at a rough understanding of atoms and electrons and how chemistry *worked*. It was a revelation, and I pored over the *Encyclopaedia Britannica* for all I could find out about the private lives of the elements, and their reactions one with another. By the age of 12 I'd managed to grasp the structure of the Periodic Table, and could always earn a half-crown by reciting its 90 odd elements off pat.

Yet the experiments I began performing in the green-house lab didn't have much connection with this elegant theory, or with any voracious desire to understand the world. I was more interested in whether I could pull them off. 'Performed' is the precise word: they were pieces of private theatre, of legerdemain. My laurel-draped hermit-age was a perfect setting, and its gothic trappings were part of the magic. The interior had been washed with slaked lime just like the tomato frames, and a jar of lime was amongst the first bottles on the shelves. My ambition was to decorate the whole room with a display of the fantastic variety of matter. I begged household chemicals from Mum and stored them in jam and mayonnaise jars, regardless of whether I was likely to find a use for them. Table salt, vinegar, washing soda (the last two – acetic acid and sodium carbonate on my fastidious labels – produced carbon dioxide when mixed) were joined by Epsom salts, lumps of chalk from the garden and borax. We were given eyebaths of this at home, but I didn't discover anything to do with it until I was in the sixth form. (In a hot flame it would fuse with metallic oxides to give brilliantly coloured 'borax beads', one of the basic procedures of analytical chemistry). Nonetheless, 'sodium tetraborate' was too impressive a label to pass by.

I shopped around the local chemists when I needed more sophisticated raw materials. Boots would supply almost anything one needed, including the apparatus, which exhausted most of my pocket money. It was exquisitely collectable stuff – beautifully polished beakers and retorts, funnels, spatulas, rubber tubing, glass tubing that you could bend and sometimes blow into small flasks over the kitchen gas. Chemicals came by the ounce in little paper envelopes, mostly from the pharmaceutical shelves. Medicinal Flowers of Sulphur heated in a crucible with iron filings made iron sulphide, which, with an acid, produced the wonderfully outrageous smell of hydrogen sulphide. Phenolphthalein (used in laxative prescriptions) went through a dramatic colour change when a solution passed from acid to alkaline, and was sensitive to a single drop. I bought acids, inflammable magnesium ribbon, all kinds of mildly toxic chemicals, even mercury (though I also filched minute quantities of this from school, since one could carry the heavy globules – as mobile as small ferrets – in one's pocket).

It was the spectacle of these transformations that intrigued me. The orange crystals called potassium dichromate would produce lurid pigments when mixed with lead and zinc salts and various combinations of acids. Some were insoluble and could be separated out on filter papers. The soluble ones appeared after evaporation in special flat earthenware dishes. Some crystals, especially alum and copper sulphate, could be grown into structures like quartz or strings of coral by cooling a saturated solution.

Generating gases seemed like alchemy (and I wasn't above collecting some personal gases, by stealing a jar sealed with a greased, ground-glass plate, into the bath one day). Just passing a current through water split it into its component gases. My apparatus for this was improvised in the best family tradition: an old aquarium cut down to bowl size, containing one copper electrode and one zinc, the latter made from one of the flexible metal tags used to hold the greenhouse roof glass in place. When they were wired up to the hand-cranked dynamo and covered with water they would fizz with fine streams of oxygen and hydrogen bubbles. Collected in jars and, burned carefully together, they turned back into water, one of the miraculous reactions that underpinned life itself.

Oddly, perhaps, I never did any experimentation with raw materials from the Field, or saw any connection between the practicalities of our days out there and the transformations in my test tubes. With hindsight, they look like very similar adventures, a search not for ways of mastering nature, but of cracking its codes, and being allowed in to watch.

3

I was, in those early adolescent years, becoming more adventurous in the countryside, too. My father had given me his black Hercules bicycle, and during the holidays I began to explore the country beyond the Field. I carried small picnics in an ex-Home Guard haversack, and did my best to ignore the hazards of being out of the home range. One problem was that nature seemed to have decided to explore *me*. I had begun to be plagued by a florid (but entirely benign) assortment of psychosomatic complaints to do with being what was quaintly known as 'highly strung'. Most of their names had the same ring of Victorian hysteria. I was prone to 'bad nerves', 'bilious attacks', what my parents called 'acidosis' (but which was just indigestion), and, most infuriatingly for a would-be open air adventurer, to hay-fever. The other hazard was more solid. The working countryside beyond the Field was peppered with short-tempered farmers and keepers, and ever since one had deliberately smashed a lovingly-built model aeroplane that had strayed into his wheatfield, I had privately declared war on them. I became resigned to meeting armed men in woods, and to the stomach-turning sound of a Land Rover stopping abruptly, changing direction and then heading inexorably towards me. Often I was caught too far from tracks and roads to have any way of escape, and stubbornly but not very sensibly used to stand my ground.

One day I set out, like Stanley, to trace the course of a river, the stream which flowed through the centre of the town and eventually joined up with the Bourne Gutter (the winterbourne) at Bourne End. I found its source two miles outside the town, an oozing field-corner next to a car dump. Feeling rather mortified, I sat on a lock by the canal and ate my egg sandwiches, hours early. Later, trying to pad out the story for friends, I made much of the mysterious quality of the puddle, how it seemed to spread about the field without any obvious edges, and how strange it was that a whole river could emerge from such an unremarkable source.

But it was the expedition itself that really mattered, the oiling and polishing of the bike, the studious poring over the map, the sense of a destination at the end of the road, with its own name and special aura. The source of the Bulbourne was at a hamlet called the Cow Roast, which was a corruption of Cow Rest, a halt on a drover's route. But I wasn't interested in these musty etymologies. To me place-names were simply codes, passwords not to the past but to the vividly present sensations of *foreign parts*. They meant new smells – of pine woods, stackyards, unfamiliar roads, which had tangs as distinctive as other people's houses; new people too, out walking, and dressed so oddly in some of the better-off quarters of the parish that they might have been in folk costume. Not everyone was so visible. The country-side was as full of signs and portents as the town – tramps' fires, names chalked on tree trunks, cryptic patterns of twigs on the paths.

In this crab-like way I began to piece together a picture of the countryside beyond the narrow parish of school. Bul-beggars' Wood (its name still puzzles me) was a copse about half a mile to the east of my house, small but made sinister by an ominously deep pit, and by lying alongside a narrow, high-banked lane. Tunnel Field was a vast, rough pasture spread out beyond the railway to the west (and once a kind of colony of our Field). There was the Italian Wood, planted by PoWs; a mist-filled valley called Soldiers' Bot-tom, where the ghosts of Cromwell's Ironsides were sup-posed to march in winter dusks; and any number of Dells and Dells Woods. I rather wish I had known then that these were corruptions of 'Devils' as often as indications of holes in the ground.

Velvet Lawn, a local recreation ground, was a rather dif-ferent case, important not in itself but because it was the gateway to a tract of parkland and wood at the top of our road. This was the Thomas Coram Foundling Hospital estate, whose boundaries were marked by dark iron posts half-hidden in the hedge, and engraved with the oddly touching and welcoming symbol of a lamb with an olive branch in its mouth. It was enticing country. 'Just off to the Top,' I'd shout back through the door at home, the short-hand registering that the place was already familiar and soon to become as important as the Field.

I'm not exactly sure how or when birdwatching became a part of these outings. My sister Pat, six years older than me and a diligent member of the Junior Bird Recorders Club, had a lot to do with it. We would sometimes bike together to Tring Reservoirs, haunt of herons and kingfishers, and the site where Julian Huxley had charted the elaborate courtship display of the great crested grebe back in the thirties. I imagine Pat showed me waders and warblers, too, but it was to be years before I got the hang of these.

The birds which mattered then were those that marked special moments of the year, or special spots. Watching them was like sharing in a secret seasonal rite. In the Christmas holidays a green woodpecker would always spend a few days on our lawn, dragging patterns through the dew with its fanned tail, and sipping ants with a tongue so pink and serpentine that we could see it from our back room. Later in the winter, if the canal iced over, moorhens would come up to the garden and pick about in the unfrozen earth under the shrubberies. In spring, my talisman was the swift, and I used to tramp up to cricket at the beginning of the summer term gazing skywards, clutching my blazer collar, and praying that I would catch my first glimpse of those careering crescent wings on the first day of May. It was a personal superstition, made up on the spot, but I was sure it would mean good luck.

Soon, growing a little more sophisticated, a few of us would comb the local woods at the start of the Easter holidays for singing chiffchaffs. There was nothing especially romantic or spring-searching about this to begin with. It was a competitive business, and our main aim was to push our personal dates for this earliest of summer visitors back ever further into March. I don't think I actually *saw* a chiffchaff for years; but there was something about the decisiveness of its thin, clear, two-note call, drifting down from the top of the still-bare ash trees that touched me. I had read somewhere that the first waves of summer migrants arrived in this country 'as promptly as if they were following an airline timetable'. Wheatears came on the 12th March, chiffchaffs on the 16th. I was amazed at the thought of these tiny creatures, just four inches in length, making the journey from Africa with such exactness, and I longed to see one on its 'proper' date.

I haven't been able to track down the book from which I picked up this notion, which now seems to assume a preposterous degree of tidiness for the natural world. But I still have my copy of Vera Barclay's *Joc, Colette and the Birds* (published in 1934), the book which turned me from a spotter into an avid watcher. My main reading at this age, like most of my friends', was the summer holiday adventure yarn. David Severn's novels (*Rick Afire*, *Cabin for Crusoe*, *Hermit in the Hills* – the titles say it all) were my favourites. Their storyline always followed much the same pattern. A group of middle-class country children strike up friendship with a footloose, slightly eccentric adult, and things start to happen. They make friends with gipsies and poachers, go off on expeditions in narrow boats or caravans, get in and out of trouble, and spend the whole time out of doors.

Joc and Colette was non-fiction but in the same mould. In this case the interloper is Tony Postlethwaite, a magazine illustrator in his mid-twenties, who has an accident near Colette's house (conveniently, her father is a doctor) and has to lie up there to convalesce. To pass the time he initiates Joc and Colette into the delights of birding. Within a matter of hours they are racing round the garden and the farmland beyond, making lists. Joc, predictably, 'did a bit of stalking', and Colette 'knew what birds she wanted to note down, and went to the places she knew she could find them'. The air is full of sibling rivalry, but Tony persuades them to combine their lists and respective talents and to watch the birds, not just tick them.

Reading the book again after a gap of 30 years I was surprised to find it more thoughtful than I remembered, with strong views on conservation. Joc and Colette are spared none of the details of Mediterranean bird-catching, or the killing of birds of prey in this country. 'Why are farmers such fools?' Joc asks in a rage (in 1934!). I also discovered where I must have made the acquaintance of some of ornithology's more enduring 'modern myths': that goldcrests had been seen migrating from Scandinavia on the backs of short-eared owls; that house martins sometimes walled in sparrows when they stole their nests; and, more plausibly, that there may be telepathic communication between birds in flocks. There is a poignant image in the book of flocks of chaffinches, feeding in a ploughed field and hidden from each other by the clods, yet all flying up in the same instant when they were alarmed.

They thrilled me, these stories, and though I kept lists too (and still do, marked up rather shamefacedly in faint pencil), what touched me most were these stirring tales of birds completing impossible journeys, seeing off marauders, coming through. I revered the spotted flycatchers that every year took the chance of nesting on top of a high-voltage transformer up the road (even though, sharing the dangers, I pinched one of their eggs). One spring I searched a 100-acre arable field for the lapwings' nest I knew was there, crawling on my stomach to try and get as close as possible before the birds took flight, but being quite overcome by the desperate distraction flights and soughing calls the birds put on to lure me away.

I never saw a truly rare bird, but one encounter changed the way I looked at them. I had just won a scholarship, our local equivalent of the 11-plus, which meant that I could stay on at Berkhamsted School, but my parents no longer had to pay any fees. As a reward my father bought me a pair of secondhand binoculars, and my mother a copy of one of the most lavish bird books then on the market, Richard Fitter's *British Birds in Colour*, with colour plates by John Gould. The binoculars were a revelation, a philosopher's stone that could transmute the most basic of sparrows into goldfinches. I took them everywhere, and became quite sentimentally attached to their fraying leather case, and the patches of bare metal where the matt-black paint had been worn off by someone else's hands.

One April afternoon I was walking with them along a thick hillside hedge up the Top, when I saw what I thought was a robin, dashing flamboyantly up and down from the hawthorns. I focussed the glasses on it, and was transfixed to see that it had a swaggering chestnut-red tail and a jet-black face. I tried to follow it, half creeping, half running when I thought it couldn't see me, trying all the while to peer through the eyepieces. It was swooping down to the ground for insects and then returning to a low branch, where it stood sentinel, flicking its gaudy tail. I felt sure I knew what it was, and when I finally lost sight of it I raced off in a state of high excitement to look up 'redstart' in my new book. There, among the thrushes, was John Gould's portrait of one in an alder tree, glowing the colour of red-hot iron, and my bird to the life. But I was perplexed by the text. 'The redstart,' it said, 'is mainly a summer resident, arriving from Africa in April . . . essentially a woodland bird, nesting in holes in trees, it is by no means con-spicuous, despite its tropically bright, burnished copper plumage, being always on the move amongst the foliage.' There wasn't much old oak woodland where I'd seen the bird. Had it been off course, or more excitingly *on* course, bound for one of its strongholds in the remote upland woods of Wales or the Lake District, using an ancestral fly-way that took it (from Africa!) through this narrow valley, *my* valley? If so, the facts that our paths had crossed wasn't just a random coincidence. The redstart and I had found the point where our territorial beats crossed, and for that fleeting moment the world had seemed a wholer and more comprehensible place.

This may not have been just an adolescent flight of fancy. In the year in which I am writing, I was walking up the same hedge on what must have been almost the same mid-April date, and saw in the distance a brown bird dart up into the hedge with that unmistakably cocky, flirting flight. I did not even need to use field-glasses this time. A male redstart in spanking new plumage allowed me to get within ten yards, just as, in a little vignette of colour and season, the last wintering redwing flew down the hedge the other way. I have seen many redstarts in the beech and birch-woods beyond the common, but this is only the second I have seen in my home range since that first bird in the self-same hedge 30 years before.

4

'Up the Top' became one of those catch-all descriptions. It was the valley of the winterbourne, the route to games or an afternoon's birdwatching, and eventually a synonym for almost any kind of outing in a vaguely southerly direction. But in my early teens it stood for a more specific walk, a circular stroll from home that could be done in half an hour but which meandered through a patchwork of woods, commons and old hedges. It began on the plateau at the top of the hill where a narrow lane struck out for the valley. My route followed this for a few hundred yards, beside a cornfield full of poppies and grey partridges, then turned left at the ridgeway through a narrow strip of common woodland (the best site for early chiffchaffs). For half a mile I kept the winterbourne to my right, and sometimes spotted owls down in its valley. Then I turned for home, back along the other side of the cornfield, past a row of great field oaks, through a bluebell copse and finally the steep pasture that lay at the very top of the Field.

I took this walk three or four times a week, and soon I was following not just a regular route but my own previous footsteps. I would keep to the right-hand side of the lane, close to a blackthorn hedge, cut a corner by an immense beech tree, and head for home along the edge of the cornfield rather than on the path a few feet below it. I think this obsessive quality was partly just a relic of childhood superstitions, like avoiding paving cracks. But I also found something reassuring in keeping to my own tracks, a sense of holding the precarious world of adolescence together. Years later I found something similar in one of William Hazlitt's essays: 'I can saunter for hours, bending my eye forward, stopping and turning to look back, thinking to strike off into some less trodden path, yet hesitating to quit the one I am on, afraid to snap the brittle threads of memory.'

At home we had a whole assortment of lighthearted euphemisms for walking. 'Just off to stretch the legs' was a favourite, or 'going for a blow' or an 'airing' – as if one was a piece of stale linen. Often that was all there was to a walk round the Top. But familiarity was making it into a personal arena, a place I knew well enough (better than *anyone*, I reckoned) to use as a secure backdrop for the more difficult bits of teenage business. I used it for earnest perambulating debates with friends – and also, absurdly, as somewhere to hide from them. When I was barred from the company of my first serious girlfriend (her father thought my political leanings were a bad influence), I used to bury messages for her under one of the landmark oaks. I revised for exams along it, with a pocketful of record cards on which I'd condensed all the topics which I was nervous of forgetting. Mostly these were to do with science, and I would tramp through whole series of bizarre conjunctions, finding myself rehearsing the violent character of the halogen gases between stolid beech trees or the equations linking momentum and mass lying on my back in the corn. Sometimes, I took a portable radio with me, to catch the King's College Carols or, aptly, the Proms.

I was, I think, beating various kinds of bounds on these ritual plods, checking both the external parish and what I felt inside. But like all well-trodden paths, it almost became a rut. One warm June evening, aged 17, I was meandering along the track doing some last-minute physics revision, the Laws of Action and Reaction, or something of that sort. Halfway through the narrow wood I saw the girlfriend of one of my old Field companions coming towards me. She was a dark, intense girl, rumoured to come from a gipsy family and to be *living* with my friend, something quite awe-inspiring then. I smiled awkwardly and she stopped, and pointing to the edge of the wood said in a beguiling Irish lilt, 'Would you be so kind as to pick some of those poppies for me?' The flowers in question were no more than ten yards away and I was convinced that, for the first time in my life, I was being propositioned. I panicked, groped for the only excuse I could think of – 'I'm sorry I have an exam tomorrow' – and scuttled off for cover along the path, scanning my fistful of cards furiously.

This ludicrous response, which seemed to make the girl as confused as me, was chiefly just a piece of adolescent funk. But I might have preserved a little dignity if the encounter had happened somewhere less emotionally charged. I felt she was a trespasser as well as a dangerously fast mover. Up the Top I was, ironically, too sure of my ground – or at least too territorially selfish about it.

*

But shows of extravagant feelings were one of the obligatory duties of puberty in the late fifties. It was the time of Angry Young Men, the Campaign for Nuclear Disarmament, and rock'n'roll (or for us middle-class kids, the more acceptably folksy skiffle) – an intoxicating brew of rebellion and idealism that breached even our school walls, and fused with our more private romantic longings. We walked about with the *New Statesman* protruding from one pocket and a volume of Keats from the other. Some of us tried our hand at poetry, or wrote the first page of a novel. I fell under the spell of the nineteenth-century nature writer Richard Jefferies, and shamelessly aped his style. (I won an essay prize for one of these pastiches, but when I asked for a copy of his 'soul autobiography', *The Story of my Heart*, it had to be vetted by the staff before I was allowed to receive it.)

In this charged atmosphere, 'ambience' surrounded every significant place and moment like a layer of ectoplasm. The early Aldermaston marches had their own special aura and, crossing the Chilterns in the Easter sunshine, felt more like spring festivals than protest marches. So did London, to which, lured by the bohemian mystique of Soho, I had begun to make illicit forays after school and in the holidays. I picked and poked about the streets exactly as I did in the lanes at home, following the enticing smells of the import record shops and chop suey houses, and relishing the simple fact of being footloose in a city.

Even school had its enchanted moments. In the summer we sometimes did practical physics out on the grass quad, and I would catch sight of our class, measuring forces with long beechwood rulers and brass weights and framed against the school chapel, like academics in a Dutch painting. And on the last assembly of every summer term we sat through the solemn ritual of the reading of Chapter 13 of St Paul's Epistle to the Corinthians – 'When I was a child, I spake as a child, I thought as a child, I understood as a child . . .' Up in the gallery we of the disaffected Sixth feigned bored contempt for such obsolete, bourgeois traditions. But in truth the words struck home. They seemed like a bridge across the generations, a fleeting glimpse of the continuity of life.

It was music that orchestrated this whole hotch-potch of emotion and politics – perhaps because it largely bypassed the annoying business of finding real words for specific ideas. Music had been my chief passion at school since I was 14, and I was repeatedly warned by my housemaster that I was 'getting it out of proportion'. But I had an insatiable, indiscriminate appetite. I had helped found the school skiffle group, taught myself rough and ready classical guitar, collected 78 rpm records of nineteenth-century Romantic composers and twentieth-century English jazz bands, and joined all the school choirs. The highlight of the choral year was a combined performance of Handel's *Messiah* with the local girls' school. We rehearsed on summer evenings in the parish church, the male voices on one side of the chancel, the ranks of girls on the other, sublime in their green gingham uniforms but quite unapproachable. We sang 'All we like sheep have gone astray' across the aisle at each other as the sun tipped down through the west window and the swift packs screamed around the spire. I became besotted by a tall, high-cheekboned soprano. I never met her, but discovered her name was Faith, which made the closing phrases of Corinthians 13 ('And there abideth these three . . .') even more agonizing at the end of term.

But all this distant and probably unwholesome worshipping came to an end in 1957. A young and enterprising maths teacher joined the staff that year, and promptly set about starting a madrigal choir, which he insisted must have both male and female voices. Astonishingly his scheme was approved, and those of us who were veteran sixth-form singers were free to join.

The collaboration was a huge success, and for me, the best experience of my last years at school. The idea had seemed like a lark at first, a gratifying slap in the face of old-fashioned segregationism. But it nourished a real passion for early music and the pure joy of singing. Much of it was outdoor and very English. We sang on what was then the Third Programme, and did a concert tour of Denmark. In the term when most of the choir were due to leave, we went off to Oxford for the day, tied two punts together and sang Orlando Gibbons' *The Silver Swan* ('that living had no note') all the way down the Isis, and would no doubt have wept if we'd been a little older. At Christmas-time we sang carols from the Cowley and Cambridge carol books round the houses of teachers and parents. The carols were mostly medieval, spiced with a little Benjamin Britten, and seemed to echo ideas older than Christianity – the promise of spring in winter, the benign power of women, the magic of song itself. We had a special understanding of each other by then, picked up through our voices and musical moods, and up in the big brown porches, breathing those plaintive harmonies out of the night air, I also felt we were singing about friendship and ourselves. I had a sensation then that I have never experienced since, of being able to observe all this happening and know that it was important, and of being completely immersed in it at the same time.

No such sensitivity, alas, penetrated my reading. The fashion at school was for a rag-bag of existentialism and nature worship – William Blake, Colin Wilson, Ezra Pound, Jack Kerouac – anything incandescent or that had *feeling*. This was the buzz word – what we, the new young, possessed and what had to be ranged against the dull reasonableness and repressed emotions and (we had picked up the word from John Osborne's *Look Back in Anger*) *pusillanimousness* of our teachers and parents. There was a terrible inevitability about my own drift towards Dylan Thomas. To an impressionable teenager, he was unquestionably a *feeling* artist, sufficiently incomprehensible to remain just beyond reach, but with some tremendous lines and titles to hang on to as slogans. 'Do not go gentle'! 'The force that through the green fuse drives the flower'! 'When all my five and country senses see'! I used to recite them to myself looking out over the view from the Top.

The first September after I left school I went on a pilgrimage to Dylan Thomas' home village of Laugharne with a close friend and fellow poetaster. John was a year older than me, a better writer, and already in a serious relationship. The journey was doomed before we set off. We hitched our way down to Wales, and on the Oxford ring road were picked up by a distinguished-looking man and his family. 'What are you up to?' he asked. 'We're poets.' John stated, as if it was his nationality. 'What a coincidence,' the man replied, 'so am I.' And a lecturer in English at Oxford. We got to Hay that night, and were rather pleased not to be able to find a pub with rooms. We slept on the banks of the Wye, wrapped up in our raincoats, and breakfasted on blackberries and half a bottle of whisky.

Two days later we reached south Wales. Our last lift was with a kitten-faced, chain-smoking middle-aged Welshwoman, who took us to her home outside Laugharne, fed us bacon and eggs, and offered us 'the room above the stables'. It sounded brilliant, a garret in Dylan's motherlode. In fact it was a hay-loft, with no windows, no light and infested with rats. That night, the woman's son, a stocky young farmer, took us over to the country club where Thomas often used to drink (he had been dead for six years). We were shocked by the regulars' descriptions of him. He had been their pet performing drunk and they despised him for it. For the price of a drink he had stood on the tables and recited doggerel, not caring that he was a laughing stock.

Meanwhile the young farmer was getting as drunk as Thomas himself. He had made a killing on the one-armed bandit, and drove us home with 14 pints inside him. We cowered in the back of the swaying Land Rover sharing the last drops of our whisky and convinced that we were going to die. We didn't, and back in the pitch-black loft, drunk, relieved, but feeling bitterly betrayed, we spent half the night in a delirious game, throwing darts (we'd found a set amongst the clutter) at the invisible rats, and then at each other's feet.

The next day, a Sunday, we went down to the 'heron-priested shore'. But there were no herons, only a grey and empty Welsh estuary at low tide. In any case our hearts were no longer in it. We were disillusioned with Thomas and embarrassed by our juvenile hysteria in the loft, and agreed without too much difficulty to abort the expedition. It took us two days to hitch back to the Home Counties, barely speaking to each other, and my sharpest memory of the whole trip is the sour taste of a burned chop suey, begged out of a Chinese restaurant in Gloucester at one minute after midnight.

The expedition had exposed too many of our differences and weaknesses, and the friendship didn't survive much longer. But it was a salutary experience. It had brought a dubious god down to mortal level and given me a taste for the unexpectedness of life on the road. But more importantly, it had shown up the fatuousness (and danger) of the belief that insight could come from wallowing in pure feeling. Writing, indeed interpreting the world at all, would have to be more like birdwatching. It would need patience, reason, and an eye for significant detail as well as imagination. I suspected that it would also involve taking a sceptical bird's-eye view of myself.

The Edge

Every August in the north Norfolk village that became my second home in the sixties, they hold a marshland sports, a day of madcap and risky events of the kind you only find in the more outlandish fringes of the country. A greasy pole quivers eight feet or so over the narrow channel of tidal water that runs past the quay, and all afternoon echoes with the sickening slaps of limbs and ribs crashing on to bare wood. There is a marsh marathon (out to Blakeney Point and back over a mile of creeks and quaking mud – any combination of transport allowed) and harrowing contests in dodgy boats. The first-aid team has a busy time.

At the beginning of the eighties, I was taking a long walk along this bit of coast for the first time in a decade and caught one of the closing events in that year's tournament. It was a barrel relay over the channel, boys against girls, with no quarter given and no handicaps. I sat in the late afternoon sun to watch, pleased that the place was still standing up for its egalitarian traditions. It was an exhausting race. Each participant had to nudge a barrel across about ten yards of moving water, then swim back to start the next member off. About halfway through the boys started to edge ahead. The tide was ebbing and the muddy edges of the channel were becoming slippery. The girls were beginning to struggle with the lolloping casks, which seemed to have a mind of their own in the gathering current. Then inspiration came to their rescue. They threw all the remaining barrels in the water, jumped in *en masse* after them, and corralling them like a log jam, ferried the whole lot over in one go. It wasn't cheating so much as lateral thinking. But the boys looked shocked and humiliated. They could still have won if they had copied this move; but they seemed to decide that there was no winning a girl's way, and went on sullenly taking their barrels across one by one.

It was one of those small incidents that seemed to catch the essence of north Norfolk. The landscape was every bit as devious and demanding as I remembered it. So was the locals' willingness to 'take it on' – especially the girls' canny short cut. Only that show of masculine pique seemed out of place. It felt like a piece of chagrin, a posture, picked up from the increasing waves of inland visitors. Twenty years before I bet that the boys would have hurled in all their barrels (and probably hurled the girls in, too).

Looking back, I think it was a stroke of luck that Norfolk was the first place I got to know after those enchanted but confined landscapes of home. I could so easily have found myself in the Lake District or the Welsh marches, chasing Celtic echoes, or roughing it with the weekend beatniks on the north Cornish coast – all places which, like Laugharne, were barely visible under their crust of associations. And, it must be said, under increasing throngs of my own contemporaries who had already taken to the road, searching for an alternative Albion.

But at the end of the fifties East Anglia was an unknown country. Maps of it were covered with blank spaces and unintelligible tangles of blue. There were no motorways to it or through it, and Beeching was closing its branch railways by the month. And except for its legendary flatness, it barely figured in popular mythology either. Its interior hadn't yet become the notorious heartland of prairie farming or its coastline one of southern England's favourite areas for second homes. *Akenfield* was ten years away, and if the region had ancestral landscapes and rural cultures, they were secrets known only to its inhabitants. In my early visits I met locals who still referred to the North Sea as the German Ocean. There was nothing affected or nostalgic about this. It was an old name which still served its purpose, pointing out that *their* North Sea – familiar, treacherous and flowing, as it were, towards them, not away – was quite different from *ours*. It sounded like the kind of name that an island people would give to a sea.

I'd had one brief glimpse of the German Ocean before, and of that laconic East Coast humour that seems like self-parody on the surface but is a dig at 'furriners'' pretensions not far below. I was about 11 and on a family holiday at Skegness on the Lincolnshire coast. My sister Pat and I had been on a guided tour of the bird sanctuary at Gibraltar Point. I can remember seeing my first wheatear flaunting its white rump in the dunes, but have an even more vivid recollection of the territorial display of a glamorous and forward (my mother would have called her 'madamish') middle-aged lady. In what seemed a daring digression at the end of the tour she had started to quiz our guide about Lincolnshire men, and why they were nick-named 'yeller-bellies'. He parried her, quick as a flash, with a story that ended with a dialect quip: 'A Lincolnshire boy meets this woman' – and we all turned to gaze at the winsome questioner – 'and she asks him "Don't you yeller-bellies have sex appeal?" "God bless you no," he says, "but we do hev secks o' spuds."'

This was a rare high spot, a glimpse of adults at play, and of the intriguing power of locality. But youthful holidays seemed mostly to have been a concoction of travel sickness and indifferent boarding houses. My parents never owned a car, and for our summer holidays we would book Mr Biggs' wallowing Humber Super Snipe, and travel down to Worthing or Pevensey on the south coast. Slabs of England slid unnoticed past my window in a fug of over-polished leather and petrol fumes. The seaside was an endless round of building sandcastles and chopping up jellyfish, and I used to long for the tumult of amusement arcades.

Most summers I went to scout camp with the school troop. We often went to the Cotswolds, where an old boy of the school had an estate which he let us use. We swam in a pool in the River Windrush, and I learned to cook Sussex Pond Pudding, stuffed with whole lemons, in a billy can. Once we went to Snowdonia, where I rather recklessly climbed Cader Idris by myself. At the top I could see clear across to the Atlantic Ocean. A few days later I almost saw it at more close quarters, when a tent we had put up on top of a cliff in an overnight expedition to Barmouth blew down in a gale. But though the practical business of camping –

the woodcraft and den-building – was as intriguing as ever, there were too many echoes of school for these summer expeditions ever to feel like real adventures. Only on my last camp, in the New Forest, where I went off for a two-day hike amongst the bogs and dragonflies, did I get a sense of what a truly wild place might be like.

So, when the chance of going to East Anglia came round again, I was as ignorant of it as I was of almost everywhere else in Britain. I was 18, and spending my time with my first non-school friends, an assortment of students and kindred spirits met at local parties and CND demonstrations. Justin was one of the newest. He lived in a large house in one of the adjoining villages, and one weekend invited a gang of us to spend a weekend on his father's boat, which was moored on the north Norfolk coast. A weekend on a yacht; it sounded impossibly grand, but hard to resist. We still enjoyed the adolescent delusion that putting ourselves at the mercy of chance, even in the most trivial situations, was tantamount to making a philosophical statement. There was a game we played on Saturday nights where we endeavoured to get to previously unknown pubs by a series of random decisions (take the first possible left turn after the first person in uniform, and so on *ad nauseam*). Going to somewhere as uncharted as East Anglia seemed much the same sort of promising lottery.

There were about eight of us on that first August trip, equal numbers of young men and women. We scrabbled about in the back of Justin's Land Rover like a pack of over-excited puppies, with barely any idea of where we were going. But the landscape along our route was a revelation. I still go to Norfolk by the same road, and still find it the most excitingly staged landscape show in England. I can make some sense of the journey now, but on those first trips it was like travelling through a new continent.

There was a quite precise point in the journey where East Anglia began for us. Just out of Baldock, we turned north-east along the route of the neolithic road known as the Icknield Way. We passed a handsome Victorian maltings and

took a long left-hand bend. Then, quite suddenly, the horizon seemed to fall away. In front of us was a vista of immense chalky fields and a sky full of larks and lapwings, and
the modest prospects of the Home Counties seemed irrevocably behind us. It was a kind of portal, and on later trips
it was always just here that we would relax and know that
we were 'away'.

Soon the fields became paler and changed from chalk to
sand. Pine trees appeared in curious stunted shapes in the
shelter belts, then massed together in the sombre plantations of Thetford Forest. There was the shock of the
American nuclear bomber base at Lakenheath, with its
runways and hangars framing the derelict flint frame of
Wangford Church. On the other side of the road, in contrast to the barricaded acres of the airfield, was the great
sweep of open heather on Wangford Warren, a remnant of
the old sandy wastes of the Breckland. These bizarre conjunctions continued. Snowberry thickets, shooting estate
fences, pheasants roaming the fields – and squashed flat in
the road. Goose-farms, sugar beet sweeping up to the walls
of more medieval churches, entirely unexpected hilltop
views, snatches of brackeny commons, then the red warning signs of the MoD ranges and processions of armoured
cars appearing out of side roads. It was a landscape of occupation one minute and openness the next.

Then, just north of Fakenham, the road tacked east-
wards, and began edging more tantalizingly towards the
coast. We passed through flint villages with names that
could have come straight out of *Cold Comfort Farm* – Great
Snoring, Bale, Glandford, Field Dalling – and caught the
first whiff of the sea. Then over a ridge of sandy gravel
where the last glacier finally petered out, and on the other
side, the first sight of the saltmarshes, criss-crossed with
silver dykes and merging imperceptibly with sea and sky.

We arrived in Blakeney in the early evening in a state of
culture shock, and found the landscapes there just as disorientating as those we'd driven through. The village street
was steep and narrow, tipping down towards the quay. The

harbour channel vanished in a maze of creeks at one end, and at the other turned through 90 degrees and snaked out through the marshes to a wide harbour, known ominously as The Pit and sheltered by a shingle peninsula. We were glad to reach the boat and find some sort of topographical mooring. She was tied up at the quay, and proved to be rather less than a yacht. She was an ancient lifeboat, converted into a liveable craft by an overgrowth of cabins, and called, for reasons we were never able to fathom, *Dilemma X*. Her superstructure appeared to have been added in much the same spirit as an allotment owner builds a shed, as a series of affectionate afterthoughts, one on top of the other. She was a labyrinth of lockers and holds, of ornamental handles and crafty Heath Robinson gadgets, and ballasted by yards of railway line. I can still conjure up her smell, a dry must of sisal and bare wood, overlaid with countless oleaginous vapours that seemed to seep from every surface.

That evening we climbed up the street to one of the village pubs. The Horse was run by Walter Long, a genial but taciturn member of a famous local dynasty. His brother, Stratton, ran the chandlery and looked after most of the boaty business in the village. (The story of the police's disbelief when they stopped Stratton Long in the nearby village of Long Stratton late one night was one of the set-pieces of local mythology.) On the bar wall there were portraits of more Longs, in a photograph of a pre-war lifeboat crew. Surrounded as we were by weekend yachtsmen in pristine slops, we gawped at these bearded patriarchs, seamen of a very different order, and read off their ages from the picture's caption. The average was well over 50. On the rescue that the photo commemorated, the conditions had been so dreadful that the men's hands had frozen to the oars. We sipped our beer and felt rather out of our depth.

Back in the boat that first night we wriggled into sleeping bags and crammed ourselves like cockroaches into the handful of bunks and any other crannies we could find. All night *Dilemma* rocked back and forth on her moorings, slapping and sucking against the quay, and momentarily seeming to slide away completely. Timbers whimpered and turned in their sleep. Outside, there were the haunting calls of invisible waders flying to roost, and those of us who had never slept on a boat before had a fretful and vertiginous night. Next morning, craning to look out of my porthole on the seaward side, I was convinced that we had actually broken free and drifted out to sea. What I saw was an astonishing panorama – a mile of saltmarsh shimmering under a high tide. The whole landscape seemed to be on the move. Terns hovered feet above the water, and arrowed down for small fish. Spikes of cord-grass and sea-lavender bounced about in the current. Swirling geometric figures opened up on the surface of the water, stretched and then closed again. Even the mud seemed alive, and slid out of the ebbing water with the moist shine of a newborn animal. Out in the distance, framed against the breakers, we could just make out Blakeney Point, the shingle spit that was all that separated the harbour from the German Ocean.

It was a sight that has kept me in thrall to this coast ever since, a liberating vision of being at the edge of things. And for the next decade or so *Dilemma* served as a refuge while we played at being weekend bohemians, fishing, bird-watching, but mostly just messing about in and out of boats. In a short while East Anglia was no longer a foreign country but 'the Ankle', a rather impertinent familiarity but one that summed up what we felt about the place, sticking eccentrically out of the corner of England, and always there when we needed to go walkabout.

Most of the time *Dilemma* stayed tight on her moorings, and only a few inches of murky sea water separated us from the land. But jumping on board seemed more than just crossing a moat; it was a voyage out of territorial waters. From the security of the top deck or a languid pose in the cabin doorway, we feigned shows of nautical knowing and general disdain for the lowly hordes parading past along the quay, that would – I hope – have been unthinkable on dry land.

No doubt the passers-by held equally disparaging views of us. Once, during a particularly lively decktop party, a passing woman sent a shrivening question across our bows: 'Are you *sailing* people?' she said in the tones of a refined north-east gale. We shrugged, jigged a bit more, laughed her off. But we were actually quite unsettled and left wondering whether this qualification would have made our rowdiness more excusable or more of an outrage. We weren't sailing people or any other kind of people. We were just there, with the same kind of arbitrariness as flotsam.

Thanks largely to our host, we got on passably well with the residents. Justin was a natural mixer and leader and, since a spell doing VSO forestry in the Gambia, had developed the knack of giving orders in such a disarming way that it seemed like a breach of simple commonsense to ignore him. He knew about restaurants and the off-season for mussels, how to mend boat engines and start accounts in shops, how to *get things done*. And, as greenhorns loose in unpredictable terrain, we were happy to give in to his genial bossiness. The locals respected his qualities every bit as much as we did, and while we were on his boat, we were in credit.

The villagers rapidly put paid, too, to any lingering stereotypes we might have cherished about 'country folk'. The ones we met showed none of the fabled East Anglian reserve and deference. They were extrovert, independent, opportunist, and had memories of epic proportions. Many didn't have a single livelihood, and followed the time-honoured rural tradition of magpie occupation, picking up work where they could, depending on the seasons, the tides and whatever chances floated their way. Living in this country that is poised between land and sea, they were natural amphibians, and not many years before they would have been part of the twice-yearly migration of land-workers – out to the coast in winter to fish for the herring, 'the silver harvest', back inland in the early summer to take in the hay and wheat. (Blakeney Church, although it was more than a mile from the sea, had an extra tower with a light in it, a beacon to guide boats into the harbour.)

There were more wrinkles in the pattern now. Michael fished for mackerel in the summer, and between trips ran a tripper boat out to the tern and seal colonies on Blakeney Point. In winter he braved the low-tide mudflats to rake out lugworms for sea-anglers from the Midlands. John also helped run boats to the Point, served occasionally on the family vegetable stall on the quay and ran a little electrical repair business on the side.

Jack, who became a special friend, was in his early sixties when we first met him and seemed to have worked at everything – harvesting, verge-cutting, baking, cockle-gathering. But his supreme skill was yarning, and I think it was this which earned him – despite a rubicund appearance and jovial temper – the nickname of Crow. He told us stories by the bucketful, and it was only after I had heard versions of his supposedly first-hand narratives in other parts of the country that I realized we may have been victims of a prolonged leg-pull.

Not many years back, he confided, he had a profitable little arrangement with the local Fire Brigade. They earned bonus money when they were called out at weekends, so, for a consideration, he would start a modest blaze on Salthouse Heath, a stretch of heather and gorse on the gravel ridge above the coast that needed only the slightest encouragement to burst into flames, and then send in a 999 call. One Saturday afternoon, though, pressed by other demands on his peculiar talents, he tried to save time by raising the alarm first. Unfortunately the fire engine and accompanying police got to the site before Crow had lit the fire, and the project fell into disarray.

Or there was the time at the end of the war, when he was driving buses along the coast road past Cley and Salthouse and was astonished one morning to see a 'white-out' on the marshes. So many mushrooms had sprung up simultaneously that it was hard to see a blade of grass between them. Crow dumped his passengers, began gathering on the marsh and for the next few days used the bus to run mushrooms back to the local shops and hotels.

It hardly mattered whether his stories were true. They were myths of a kind, catching the contrary, wayward flavour of the local landscapes – and of Crow himself. He would often recount them while performing similarly tall tricks with the bar skittles. He would crouch down, sight up the ball, and send it looping out towards the tap-room door handle. Then, just as it was swinging back towards the board he would raise an arthritic leg and give it a hefty kick, sending it back the way it had come to knock the whole boardful flat.

2

Gradually we evolved our own routines and customs. On Saturday mornings we would mooch about the quay, which served as a kind of maritime village green, and then go off to Holt or Sheringham to shop. There was a chandlery at Sheringham that sold cheap slops and smelt like the primeval source of all *Dilemma's* odours, but which we chiefly revered for its name – the Great Grimsby Coal, Salt and Tanning Company. On Saturday evenings we would usually drive out to a pub in one of the nearby villages. We would follow the coast road along the edge of the marshes to Salthouse or Morston, or strike inland to Field Dalling, through the pale, airy landscape of the Norfolk Heights (a rather grand title: the highest point is 250 feet above sea level).

Our destination in Field Dalling was the Jolly Farmers, run by Charlie, who always welcomed us with great solicitude ('Here's my boys') in a gravelly, Long John Silver voice. We played darts and skittles and talked a great deal. About what I have only patchy memories, except that the conversation could slip from pacifism to the art of eating live shellfish with barely a bump, and that it was punctuated with strings of clannish puns and references. Norfolk had that effect, loosening us up, fraying the edges of things. Sometimes, driving back from Field Dalling, we would see barn owls, quartering the road verges in the light from the car headlamps.

But there were gaps in this sociable round and increasingly I began to take myself off to the saltings. I'd found the marsh landscape incomprehensible at first, too huge and incoherent to be anything other than a backdrop. But it had that twice-daily refashioning by the tide, and as I got used to its rhythms, it began to seem less foreign. A favourite spot was where the channel flowed into the Pit and the sea wall turned east towards Cley. It was only about half a mile from the quay, past the pitch where a spectacularly tanned villager nicknamed Mahogany hired out his rowing boats and canoes to holidaying children, past a beached houseboat with an uncanny resemblance to a children's book illustration of Noah's Ark. All these tripperish ornaments – the parked dinghies, the waterfowl collections and neat drainage dykes – were left behind and you stepped out on to real saltmarsh. It was a strange new substance, spongy, unpredictable, full of unfamiliar plants, broken by dark pools and glistening creeks. It seemed to grow out of the bare mud and sand, the thin films of algae glueing the surface in place, the first shoots of samphire acting like a net to the tidal wash of silt. Wherever you put your feet there was a film of flotsam caught between the plants: shells, seeds, birds' wings, bladderwrack, fish-egg cases, all coated with spindrift and plankton and waiting to be doused, ground down by the tides, turned back into mud.

A little higher up the shore, where the ground was firmer, I would sit and watch the tide coming in over this moist green pelt in something close to a trance. I'd screw up my eyes and peer obsessively for the turn, fixing on an identifiable pattern in the sand or a clump of cord-grass, and trying to spot the first signs of its disappearance. There would be no more than a sheen at first, a satining across the surface of the flats; then fingers of water, held back by their own surface tension, would push between the shallow ripples in the sand. Suddenly the tension would break and they would turn into trickles, then thin streams, until acres of previously solid land had been turned into open water. Sometimes, if the tide-race was deep enough, it could be transformed by changes in wind or cloud cover. A cat's paw breeze could turn the surface from matt-grey to the rippling purple of reed-plumes. Tide-watching became as compulsive as peering into a fire – except that here, when the ebb came, everything re-emerged, soft-edged, as good as new, but with a subtly altered geography that had never existed exactly so before.

And on to the newly exposed mud skimmed flights of wading birds to pick out the food left behind by the tide. There were redshanks and oystercatchers and many others which I didn't yet know, but their calls – urgent, fleeting, conjuring up vast distances – seemed part of the spirit of the place.

I sometimes wondered if the closeness of these unstable edges of the land was part of the secret of Norfolk's appeal to us, a reflection of a half-conscious desire to be as contingent as spindrift ourselves, to stay loose, cast off, be washed up somewhere unexpected. Down among these shifting sands the world seemed to be all possibility.

But there was nothing unconscious about our fantasies of the Point. It was our Coral Island, an enchanted oasis of lagoons and shifting sands, fanned by the coconut and honey scents of tree lupins and sea pinks. Even when rain hung over the mainland this three-mile-long peninsula often lay under its own mysteriously clear strip of blue sky. In summer we went out there whenever we could, catching the tourist ferries, sailing our own dinghy, or just trudging along the long shingle beach which joined the Point with the neighbouring village of Cley. We spent whole days there, lounging amongst the dunes. We dozed by the salt-water pools (and in them sometimes), played cricket with driftwood bats, and munched crabs we had bought in the village and dismembered with pebbles and fingernails. Sometimes we surprised seals basking on the sands, or shared a lagoon with a tern flock, raining down on the shoals of whitebait marooned there. We went gathering ourselves – picking samphire (the shoots were edible) on the mudflats or scratching for cockles where there was a likely looking film of plankton over the sand.

If the tides were right, we would go back by boat, a rhapsodical journey with the setting sun behind us and little terns diving for fish in the boat's wash. Mostly though, we would tramp round the rim of the Pit at low water. It was a slapstick, foot-testing hike, that took us through sweeps of sea-lavender and silver wormwood, into chest-deep creeks and beds of jagged flints and mussel shells, and everywhere through mud – deep, black, sucking mud with the consistency of vaseline. The deeper we sunk and the louder the clooping as we retrieved our legs, the faster adult decorum slipped away. We arrived back in the village (and sometimes, to our delight, to an audience of more upright holidaymakers) draped with edible greenery and wearing our grime like a badge of identity.

We took our food very seriously, trying to concoct meals from Elizabeth David's early Penguins and Dorothy Hartley's epic *Food in England*. They leaned towards ethnic extremes (ethnic English included), and were frequently absurdly ambitious for *Dilemma*'s four foot square galley. I flinch at the memory of the fat-laden and vaguely Moorish concoctions – mostly half-cooked in the thin flame of calor gas – that I inflicted on my friends, as a result of having watched a Tunisian chef cooking in the open air in Paris.

But the star features of our cuisine, if rarely the mainstays, were the wild foods that we had picked ourselves. It was something of a novelty at first, this idea of living off the land, but we rapidly adapted to it. Samphire was the easiest to learn about, and the strangest. The bright green shoots – half seaweed, half thornless cactus – were sold in fishmongers and in dozens of cottages along the coast road. But Crow had taught us how to pick it ourselves. You looked for shoots that had 'been washed by every tide', pulled it up by the roots, rinsed off the mud before carrying it back, but *never* let it stand in water. Crow had a recipe for pickling the stuff that he'd used when he was a baker – 48 hours under warm vinegar in a cooling bread oven. We favoured a less drastic treatment: steamed for quarter of an hour, then eaten with molten butter, a bit like asparagus, with the flesh drawn off the central spine between the teeth. The taste was a revelation – tangy, succulent, salty, full of warm hints of iodine and ozone.

Then Crow showed us wild sea-spinach, whose thick, creaking leaves sprouted along the sea walls. It tasted like a spinach which had been rescued from all the insults and emasculation of institutional cooking, and we were instant converts. We discovered fennel growing along the coastal road verges, and with it conjured up cold Russian yoghurt soups and Mediterranean sauces for mackerel. We gathered cockles, razor-shells, even limpets. Winkles, especially, were abundant out on the flats. One night we left a bucket of winkles to soak overnight in *Dilemma*'s sink, and temporarily forgot about them – until about midnight, when extraordinary rustling noises began coming from the galley. We were used to *Dilemma*'s night-time repertoire of sounds by now, but this was different. Cracks and splashes gathered in tempo, as if the timbers were being chomped by an army of small beavers. Inside the galley there were winkles everywhere, dropping from the rim of the bucket, crawling across the floor, scaling the walls. It was a touching and determined display of the survival instinct, and I am pleased that for once we overrode Justin's hard-headed counsel, gave in to sentiment and put the lot back in the sea.

Most of the foraging – particularly for samphire and mushrooms – we did as a group. We never saw anything resembling Crow's wartime mushroom 'white-out', but the grazing marshes inside the sea wall were still good hunting grounds. We usually went mushrooming in the late afternoon, ready for supper or breakfast the next day. But one day we decided to do the job properly, out at dawn as folklore decreed – though what reasoning lay behind this old saw we didn't know. Did mushrooms actually come up in the night? Did they taste better dawn-fresh, as hinted in the adverts? There certainly seemed to be more of them about that morning when we arrived at Salthouse marshes at 6 a.m., but there were also more pickers – a factor we hadn't had to consider before. They had come on to the marsh by a direct route from the road, and spent as much time glaring in our direction as they did searching for mushrooms. We guessed that they were locals, and that we had strayed into a territory that was defined as much by time as ground space. But it was clearly no more their land than ours and we stood our ground. For the next half an hour our combined movements resembled a bizarre formation dance. We never spoke, signalled or in any way acknowledged each other's presence, but somehow kept a steady 20 yards between us as we slowly quartered the marsh, sneaking hooded glances at our rivals between periods of intense scanning for the half-hidden white caps. Both parties managed to cover just about the entire marsh under this primitive but equitable arrangement, and both went back with full baskets.

They were economical and very satisfying, these spells of partial self-sufficiency, and they made more of an impression on me than I realized at the time. They also, less creditably, contributed to the heroic ideals of noble savagery to which we aspired. In retrospect there was something slightly dogged about our determination to rough it, and we often made fools of ourselves. One August weekend we arrived in Blakeney to find that *Dilemma* had been beached for painting, and was now perched at an angle of about 30 degrees at the edge of the quay car park. It was a disagreeable shock for a while, and made sleeping on the boat an even more testing geometric problem than usual. But it didn't take us long to see that our half-acknowledged dream of being a conspicuous utopian island slap in the middle of mainstream society had been realized. We ate our Sunday lunch (roast chicken and samphire, a perfect compromise) draped about the sloping deck and in full view of the day-trippers – about as comfortable as beached jellyfish but as happy as sandboys.

By the time we had been coming to Norfolk for about two

or three years we had seasonal as well as daily customs. In high summer we would sometimes take *Dilemma* up the channel and moor her in the Pit for a few days. We took some food with us, and bought fresh mackerel from the fishing boats on their way back to the quay. But there was no substitute for a landbound pub, so we would row to shore in the evenings, on to the mudflats on the landward side of the Pit, and then walk the last mile over rickety plank bridges and mud that could be as slippery as black ice. It was a precarious journey even in daylight, and we were lucky that we always managed to get back safely in the dark. Justin wouldn't allow us to use torches in case we dropped them and had a fit of night-blindness over one of the deep creeks. So if there was no moon, the only light we had was from the phosphorescent algae that bloomed in the water in the summer months. They flared like faint sparklers whe-rever they were splashed into the air. Sometimes we would see our footsteps glowing for an instant behind us in the damp sand, and small luminous fountains bubbling up if someone peed in the water. We rowed back to *Dilemma* with the tips of the oars leaving glowing arcs against the night sky.

Dilemma was in dock during the winter, but we usually managed to find a cottage to let or somewhere to stay for a few days over New Year. The winters seemed to be clearer and more decisive in those days, and walking along the sea wall to Morston or Cley we had views over miles of frosted marshes, glittering under skies of the purest, sharpest blue. We would watch short-eared owls beating over the rough grass and flocks of waders swirling like smoke over the dis-tant mudflats. Sometimes gales and flood tides would smash holes in the sea defences and turn the whole marsh-land habitat inside-out. The creeks and channels were bat-tered into new outlines. Tongues of shingle were sprayed back amongst the samphire flats and muddy pools hollowed out in the middle of the beach. In places the sea-blite bushes that grew on the margin between the beach and salt-ings were buried under tons of shingle. But by summer they had always started to reappear, the pale new shoots springing out of the tops of the buried plants and pushing their way up through two or three feet of pebbles. The tenacity of these shoreline plants was awesome. One of them, the maritime variety of the common curled dock, used its withered last-year's stems as a kind of protective tent for its new late winter shoots.

Blakeney itself had the same kind of indomitability. Every spring Stratton Long's men waymarked the new course of the channel out to the Pit by a line of tall white poles. But many of the full-time boatmen had a buccaneering attitude towards this sign-posted trail. They would edge back to the quay on the lowest possible tide and dodge through the poles where they thought they could get away with it. Their favourite trick on the last narrow reach back to the quay was to work the tiller nonchalantly with one hand and roll a cigarette ('wibbling' they called it) with the other.

Once or twice a year during the high spring tides, the seaward edge of the village flooded. The sea would come over the quay-road and start creeping up the High Street. It never reached the plaque on the hotel which marked the high point of the terrible East Coast floods of 1953, but when it began lapping on the doorstep of the knitwear shop it was reckoned to be a 'fair tide'. A few cars were always trapped in the car park and the attendant's booth sometimes bobbed free of its moorings and floated off amongst the dinghies. People who lived in the village were used to all this and there were accepted, if informal, flood routines (everyone knew, for instance, where the bus-stop moved to). The more adventurous went shopping by boat, and for a few hours the road between the tall walls of the hotel and the quay rail took on the look of a rather grand moat.   .

The sea, of course, was just reclaiming old territory. Five hundred years ago the coastline was a mile further inland, and Blakeney was a working port. Cargoes were taken down the steep street backwards, braked by horses facing up the hill. I once saw a bulldozer, clearing up flotsam after a high tide, slide gracefully over the edge of the quay and into the water, turned into something rather less than horseflesh by the landscape. The driver looked at what had happened, got out of his cab and walked slowly back up the hill for a pint.

3

During the mid-sixties Norfolk's star waned a little. *Dilemma* passed to one of Justin's relatives and eventually suffered the indignity of having her endearingly ramshackle top-quarters sawn off, trimmed to family cruiser size. It was the kind of fate that looked like overtaking many of us. I'd come down from university, done a spell teaching liberal studies in a further education college, and in 1966 ended up as an editor in Penguin Books' educational division. It was hardly a nine-to-five job, but there weren't those same endless expanses of vacation time available. I was beginning to dabble in journalism, too, doing reviews for the educational press and the odd political piece for magazines. In the heady atmosphere of the sixties, Norfolk and the marshland birds seemed a world away, an indulgence which was verging on the frivolous.

Ironically, it was during the tumultuous spring of 1968, when Paris went up, the anti-Vietnam war protests reached their peak, and even Penguin got caught up in the student risings, that I was struck by a pang to be up to my knees in mud and listening to the tideline waders again. I don't know why this should have happened just then. One of the odd features of the events of 1968 was that though they contained the germ of the Green movement, they were played out in uncompromisingly urban settings (we missed out on that splendid Parisian slogan, 'Beneath the pavement the beach'). Perhaps that was the problem. Perhaps things were a little too exuberant, a kind of spring fever, and there was a need for space in which to cool down in. Whatever the reason, the Ankle, as usual, seemed just the right kind of haven, a place to reset the sails, maybe a corner of the promised land already.

Something of the same hankering had struck an old birding and college friend, Peter Newmark, and in the last week of April we took off on a whim for the Norfolk coast. We booked into a draughty boarding house in Cley, run by an eccentric family who received us standing to attention in a row, like old retainers. That evening an east wind got up and began shaking the house, making it seem even more like the location of some comic horror film. Peter and I made our excuses after supper and fled out to the coast road. It was a wild black night as we gazed out over the invisible sweeps of Cley and Salthouse marshes, where we were bound in the morning. They had the reputation of being one of the best birdwatching sites in Britain, and after a good blow right in the middle of the great spring movements, almost anything could turn up.

The next day it rained non-stop, a thin, bitter, spirit-sapping drizzle driving in from the sea. We made a mental apology to all those Blakeney trippers we'd once mocked for picnicking deep in their saloons, parked the car opposite one of the roadside pools, and settled down to watch the waders in comfort. With occasional bursts from the windscreen wipers it proved to be a rather effective and commodious hide. We picked out redshanks and greenshanks feeding on the edge of the mud (20 yards didn't even make Peter's red-green colour blindness a problem), and after rummaging in our Collins Field Guide and craning out of the side windows for glimpses of white rumps, sorted out green and common sandpipers. The illustrations in the guide were by a man called R.A. Richardson and we rather took to them. He had caught the waders especially well, preening and probling in lively, upright poses.

The next morning, a Saturday, was bright and dry, and we drove over to Cley's East Bank, a broad sea wall that divides the freshwater reedbeds and marshes from the saline lagoons, and the main lookout station for birders. People decked out with impressive assortments of optical equipment paraded back and forth along the top, and one of them – a stocky figure in his mid-forties, dressed in denims and dark blue bobble hat – greeted us as he left. 'Morning. Purple heron in the reedbeds if you haven't seen one before.' It was said with disarming casualness, as if we were old friends and purple herons everyday occurrences. Then he jumped on an immense Norton motorcycle and roared away.

Peter and I shuffled up the bank feeling as awkward as if we had turned up for a première in the wrong clothes. How was one supposed to behave in a place where such exotic birds (I hadn't even *heard* of purple herons at the time) just dropped in, amongst people who had no trouble in recognizing them? But it wasn't hard even for us to spot the bird. Its rust-coloured neck was protruding out of the reeds about 40 yards from the path, cryptic and motionless, as is a heron's way. It was also at the focal point of about a score of binoculars and telescopes. The watchers sprawled on the bank were chatting about the heron's likely origins ('Overshot from Holland probably. Came in when the pressure rose') and of their own glamorous sightings on Fair Isle and Scilly. We kept mum about our triumphs with the shanks. But we did learn that the man who'd spoken to us in the car park was none other than Richard A. Richardson, bird artist and man of Cley extraordinary. We opened the book at his picture of the heron. It was an oriental-looking bird, with slanting yellow eyes and pigtail crest, its bronze and black striped neck merging into a darkly mottled body. Our chance encounter made the illustration take on an awesome authority; this man was *steeped* in purple herons.

Later he returned to the bank, and we managed to find a space in the admiring throng that settled at his feet. It was perfect weather for migrants, with a warm southerly breeze blowing in over the German Ocean. The marsh hummed with life. There was a constant stream of new arrivals and birds stopping off for refreshment on the pools. Richard seemed to be able to magic them out of the air. He sat on the bank like the conductor of an orchestra and in they came, on cue. Black terns, already in sooty summer plumage, wafted up the dykes and dipped as they passed him. A nod of the bobble hat towards the reeds and they were full of dithering bearded tits, chiming like muffled bicycle bells. A flip of the binoculars – they were small and held between the finger and thumb of one hand, like opera glasses – and up at the back of the marsh rose two black-tailed godwits, the first of these beautiful chestnut and grey wading birds to nest in Norfolk since the early nineteenth century.

The godwits' triumphant flights over their reclaimed territory that morning turned into a cadenza, a heart-lifting display of virtuosity and nerve. They rose up as high as larks, wings fanning furiously, long bills arched upwards until, at the top of the climb, they softened like windblown paper, flapping slowly and teasingly and calling an insistent, echoing seesaw note that carried half a mile across the marsh in spite of the clamour of the gulls.

Then suddenly there were four godwits, about more urgent business. A big female Montague's harrier, Britain's rarest bird of prey, had come prowling in from the west. It coasted just above the top of the reeds, as buoyant as a will 'o the wisp, with its wings feathered just above the horizontal. Sometimes it vanished along a dyke, but we were able to follow its path from the wake of mobbing and screaming birds behind it. It was hunting frogs, birds' eggs, voles – anything small that it might catch unawares. The godwits weren't in danger, but they went for the harrier like a fighter wing. They towered up from the marsh in V-formation. They looped over it, dived at it, rose up again in a wave, never breaking that lopsided arrow formation. All the while Richard was keeping up his laconic commentary, a mix of godwit's-eye jokes, anecdotes of harriers past, and speculations about the meaning of what was going on in front of us. He talked about mobbing as a kind of cooperative hue and cry, which warned other birds of danger, and speculated that the bravura performance by the godwits was probably a sign that they were young birds, perhaps first-time breeders. More experienced adults often lay low

71

when predators were about.

Peter and I watched the sun go down from the same spot where we'd huddled inside the car the previous day. In the distance we could see the harrier roosting on a post against a thronging panorama of birds. I felt I was back inside Norfolk again, not just observing it from the outside. There was something new, though, a feeling that this was a *community* of living things, feeding, breeding, struggling for space but ultimately supporting each other, and that humans could be part of this, but only on terms set by the landscape.

Within a few weeks I'd made the decision. I wanted a base of my own here, and to hitch some part of my livelihood to it. My work at Penguins wasn't tied to an office, and much of the time spent planning or reading manuscripts could be done anywhere. I'd also had a brainwave for a book of my own – on the edible wild plants that we'd begun to learn about on *Dilemma*. I imagined myself taking long weekends and holidays up here, birdwatching in the mornings, plant-hunting in the afternoons and retiring to Penguin work in the evenings. I would be living *on* Norfolk as well as in it.

And that, for once, was exactly how it worked out. Walter Long had a cottage to let in Blakeney High Street, just a few yards up from his pub, and with a three-year lease. It was perfect, a converted slaughterhouse with three floors that could sleep eight people at a pinch. It also had an extraordinary window between the kitchen and sitting room, more like a small proscenium arch than a serving hatch, and an irresistible temptation to ongoing theatrical banter between parties camped out in the two rooms. 'Sixty-nine A' soon became as popular a weekend retreat as *Dilemma* had been.

At other times I would stay up by myself and slip into that tidal regime I had dreamed of. In the mornings I would cycle the two miles over to Cley for an hour or two with Richardson's informal class on the East Bank. He was a creature of strict routines and arrived on the bank at 10 a.m. each morning. He came on foot for this first visit of the day, accompanied by his two arthritic Yorkshire terriers, but always wore much the same combination of motor-cyclist's leather and denim in which I'd first met him. They were like ornithological *salons*, those morning sessions. About half a dozen of us would settle down on one side of the bank, gazing out east over the saline pools of Arnold's Marsh, identifying feeding waders and tuning in to the flight calls of overhead migrants. Then we would all slide across to the other side of the bank, survey the reedbeds and grazing marshes to the west and repeat the performance.

Richard would sit there, a cross between Mr Punch and a weatherbeaten rocker, rolling minutely thin cigarettes, doing outrageous and often libellous impersonations of other birdwatchers, and raising his binoculars occasionally (though he barely needed them) to verify a wader flying in half a mile away. He had natural long sight and an astonishing ability to recognize birds by their 'jizz', a skill which he was always happy to share, without the slightest hint of patronization, even with extreme novices. But he would not tolerate pedants and posers, and was regularly involved in bitter skirmishes with the local landowners whenever they presumed to know more about the workings of the marsh than he did. He was nearly always proved right in the end.

I got to know Richard a little over the years that followed, but he never talked about his private life, or indeed much about his painting. But the rumours were exotic. He had been born in London, the illegitimate son of a seaman, had spent his youth in an orphanage and been introduced to Norfolk in his twenties by a well-to-do lady who'd seen some of his sketches. He'd lived in the same digs in Cley ever since. He was entirely self-taught as a painter, but made an acceptable living from his book illustrations and from commissions picked up on the East Bank. He had published one book of his own, the austerely named *Checklist of the Birds of Cley*, but in a way he was himself the Book of Cley. His knowledge of local natural history was so ex-

73

haustive and idiosyncratic that it assumed the status of an alternative parish history. Like the country doctor in John Berger's *A Fortunate Man*, Richard was the unofficial clerk of the records and knew more than most of the village's life-long residents about its social and geographical quirks.

But it was his uncanny knack of being able to see the world from a bird's point of view that was his special gift. He could turn migrating golden plovers and whimbrel round in the sky by whistling their contact calls, and predict from which invisible spot ground-nesting birds would fly up. I remember his gazing at a flock of terns wafting in to fish in the pools, and saying simply, 'It would be worth a skua's while . . .' It was. A minute or so later an Arctic skua, a dark, piratical snatcher of other birds' fish, slid in over the sea wall and began harrying the terns. He seemed to have been blessed with a sixth sense, a bond with the natural world that nonetheless never lent him the slightest touch of folksiness. Once, he sauntered on to the bank with a portable tape recorder, sat down and turned it on without a word. On the tape were the poignant, liquid flutings of a golden oriole, one of the rarest and most glamorous of the casual migrants that turned up in Norfolk. Of all the places on the Norfolk coast it had chosen Richard's garden in which to touch down, and had burst into song on a perch right outside his bedroom window.

In the afternoons I would go foraging, after stories and raw materials for the book I was planning on edible wild plants. I had the title – *Food for Free* – and knew exactly the angle I wanted to take. It wasn't going to be a guide to survival or 'self-sufficiency', or, at the other extreme, a folksy cookbook. Norfolk and begun to stir the idea that there were natural communities and that humans could have relationships with them that did not necessarily involve domination or 'management'. I wanted to try and catch this feeling at a matter-of-fact level, to re-enact, through examples readers could try for themselves, the inventiveness and intimacy which people once had with wild food plants – and were still occasionally forced back on, in times of hardship. It felt a good time for such a book, too, with the first glimmers of ecology beginning to surface.

It was a Norfolk man, the eighteenth-century Yarmouth cobbler and schoolmaster Lilly Wigg, who wrote the first treatise on 'esculent plants' and there was no shortage of edibles in the county. But, except along the coast, the knowledge about how to use them seemed to have slipped out of folk memory. I had to gather clues from old herbals and cookery books, and trust that they weren't too mistaken. Often I worked from a kind of presumption of innocence, assuming that anything not actually described as poisonous might be worth a try, especially if it was related to a known edible.

Everyone visiting the cottage was recruited into the business of foraging and testing. We would comb the coast for sea-kale and wild cabbage, and anything vaguely promising in the spinach line, sometimes having to improvise driftwood and twine frames to carry the bundles home. We harvested berries and fungi inland, especially the delectable giant puffballs that spring up like huge displaced eggs under the hedges in September. Sixty-nine A's kitchen turned into an experimental station, forever full of jars of pickle and strings of drying herbs.

But it was samphire – glasswort, pickle-plant, crab grass, the first opportunist colonizer of the mudflats and a species that grew in places as thickly and generously as grass – which remained our staple and our totem. We found all kinds of new ways of eating it – stuffed in lamb, tangled up with spaghetti, stir-fried with dabs. We munched strips of it raw as thirst quenchers when we were walking on the marshes. And we heard Crow's tale of the monster specimen that had sprung up near the local sewage outfall after the 1953 floods, when all kinds of unconventional fertilizers had been washed into the creeks. It was six feet tall and as thick as a leek at the base. It was carried back to Blakeney tied to the crossbar of a bike, and later hung above the bar of the White Horse, like a prize fish.

It was one of Crow's more outrageous stories, yet as so

often it held a kernel of insight. Plants here weren't just botanical specimens or members of a species. They were also individuals, with a past. They figured in our mental maps of north Norfolk. Fennel wasn't just *Foeniculum vulgare*; it was a relic of Roman cuisine, the tall colonies by the side of the road to Morston, a first flash of feathery aniseed-scented foliage in May. It wasn't cultivated but it was part of our culture.

Sadly, the cottage proved a shade too agreeable. I became more involved with Penguin and found it hard to get away, even for weekends. Friends (and eventually strangers) with fewer obligations were more than happy to keep it warm. It was a sensible use for an otherwise empty property, but the place didn't feel like mine any more, and when the lease was up I didn't renew it. When I next came back to north Norfolk, it was with a different group of friends on another stretch of the coast.

But I go back to Blakeney from time to time. I still follow the same route, past the airfields and the squat pines, and along the road from Fakenham that edges so slowly towards the coast. I drive to Morston, run out on to the mud, try to whistle at the passing whimbrels and gaze out at that thin blue line that hangs over the edge of the Point.

Part Two:
The Knowledge

1

The job at Penguin marked the beginning of a different phase in my life in which – appropriately perhaps – glimpses of history and other people's writings about landscapes began, at last, to make a mark on me.

It also proved to be the gateway to landscapes very different from north Norfolk and the Chilterns, not least to the bizarre surroundings of the office itself. Our department was perched on the side of a canal in West Drayton, a couple of miles from the firm's headquarters near London's Heathrow Airport and in a hinterland of rubbish dumps, quarries and undeveloped wasteland. The whole district felt transient and precarious. Things happened on the surface (and disappeared underground, one suspected) that would never be tolerated in city centres or open countryside. A field would be a sour paddock one month, a car breaker's yard guarded by chain-link fencing and Alsatian dogs the next, and end up as a prefab paint factory. To the west, the landscape frayed like an old sponge into a maze of flooded gravel pits and stagnant feeder canals. Our building shared in the general atmosphere of shiftlessness. It was wedged between the canal and main road, a thin triangle that from the outside looked as insubstantial as a film set.

It ought to have been a depressing backcloth. But the late sixties was an exhilarating time to be buzzing about on the fringes of the education system and, on the days when our location did seem a little tawdry, it simply seemed to heighten the challenge of the job. The education division had been set up by Penguin's founder, Sir Allen Lane, with a brief to try and give educational textbooks the same populist shot-in-the-arm that Pelican paperbacks had given general non-fiction in the thirties. We had been allowed three clear years for research and development, without any need to make a profit – a luxury that would be inconceivable now – and we happily worked long hours. We toured schools and colleges, talked to teachers, sat in on classes and explored how the new discovery methods and cross-disciplines might be translated into book form. We worked with the pupils too (it was the time – equally remote now – when children, not their parents, were seen as the real customers of the education business), trying to get a measure of their sophistication and expectations in reading matter. We tracked down real writers with a commitment to education and linked them up with sympathetic schools. Back in the office we planned majestic projects, mocked-up pages, and had ceaseless debates about it all, which in the evenings spilled over to the pub across the road. I think all of us would have relished those years even if we had been holed up in a cellar.

As it was, the setting for the West Drayton film lot proved to be anything but dispiriting. Nature seemed to have caught the mood of the times, and the whole area was brimming with rowdy, opportunis life forms. Just looking out of the window provided a daily dose of optimism. I could watch wintering grey wagtails bobbing about on the polystyrene debris floating in the canal, or water voles dodging under the banks. In the summer the towpaths and thin seams of land between factory walls and water were decked with wetland flowers – purple loosestrife, skullcap, gipsywort. House martins nested above the door of the pub, and the patch of waste ground that lay between the office and the canal bridge was the hunting ground of our local kestrel. It would hover motionless over the early evening traffic jams, sliding a few feet to one side, flicking its wings and fanned tail for balance, hanging still again, its field of view going beyond the lava flow of traffic to the teeming vegetation at the back of the towpath It would, in a way, have been an apter mascot for us thar the juvenile Penguin on our notepaper.

Soon I was exploring further afield in the lunch break, squirming through broken corrugated fences and finding myself in terrain that defied all the conventional ways of categorizing land. About half a mile from the office the canal ran alongside the remains of a defunct refuse tip. It was third generation wasteland here: one-time gravel diggings, later filled in with rubbish, now returning to scrub and young woodland. In summer the open patches were covered with plants springing from domestic garbage: tomatoes, sunflowers, fennel, and throw-outs from the herbaceous beds. And in one corner, amongst piles of half-buried dark blue and green Victorian bottles, something more sinister – a sprawling, jagged plant with elegant white trumpet flowers and large fruits, like thick-spined conkers. I recognized it as thornapple, a highly toxic member of the nightshade family, but had no idea how it had got here. Back home I read up its history. It was a native of Peru, brought to Britain in the sixteenth century as an all-purpose narcotic, asthma cure and aphrodisiac. (One herbalist described how 'wenches give half a dram of it to their lovers, in beer or wine. Some are so well skill'd in dosing of it that they can make men mad for as many hours as they please'). Its seeds usually arrived in Britain as impurities in bags of South American fertilizer. They could stay dormant under the soil for at least a century, and this specimen, sprouting amongst the medicine bottles, might just have been a relic of the time it was still being cultivated as a drug plant.

The maps I had of this part of Middlesex didn't do justice to these accidental corners. The landscape changed too quickly to be chartable. But I learned what were the likely spots, the white gaps in otherwise densely occupied areas (wasteland is sometimes called 'white land' by planners), the hatching that represented the edges of old tips, the railway sidings and shunting yards and ragged-edged gravel pits. With the help of friends who lived locally I tracked down pits where great crested grebes nested on discarded car tyres; a canal aqueduct where swallows swooped over what was, in effect, split-level water; and the sewage farm at the end of the main runway at Heathrow, where migrant waders stopped off to feed in the sludge. Even the coach journey to work became an event one summer when a colony of sand martins nested in a sandy bank scalloped out during the building of a new roundabout. When the young were out they whirled about the traffic like confetti.

I was fascinated by the tolerance and resourcefulness of these creatures in exploiting, *naturalizing*, human habitats. They seemed to be saying something about survival and the possibilities of co-existence that was worth recording. The story became a book called *The Unofficial Countryside*. The irony was that this maverick, improvised habitat insisted on my working according to its own rules. I tried organizing the book around a long safari through the urban outback, but lost touch with its surprise and spontaneity. I found in the end that a record of happenstance discoveries on lunch-hour strolls, serendipity on the railways, birds glimpsed through windows, caught the flavour of these informal (and often short-lived) landscapes much more truthfully.

The book led to a television film, made with David Cobham, which took the whole of Greater London as its catchment area and revealed even more dramatic examples of natural opportunism. We filmed kestrels nesting in tower-block window boxes and foxes hunting in cemeteries. We found giant hogweed, a vast umbellifer from the damp regions of the Caucasus which had enjoyed a brief popularity in Victorian gardens, escaping to form feral colonies in the boggy surrounds of the Hoover factory. And in the derelict shell of Beckton gasworks in the East End we filmed black redstarts (scarce relatives of the common redstart I had watched as a teenager at home) which normally haunt the low mountain slopes and stone villages of southern Europe. They began colonizing Britain just after the last war, and seemed to find the moraine of a blitzed city an agreeable substitute for their natural rocky habitats. In Beckton their thin metallic songs echoed amongst the empty gasholders as if they had been made for the place.

In some places the fit between wild creatures and artificial habitats was uncanny. It was exactly as if a parallel universe was inhabiting the same space as us, living independently but learning to use our trade and our surplus energy and food for its own purposes. Down at the Ford works in

Dagenham we located a colony of tumbleweed, whose seeds had hitched a lift into Britain in the packing cases of engine parts from the United States. They had found their way to the company rubbish tip, and had germinated and flourished in the layers of hot ash that were raked out of the foundries each week. The day we had permission to film at the factory, a wind got up and the tumbleweeds began rolling, whipping up dust as they passed the saloon cars in their high security enclosure, Dagenham suddenly transformed into Dallas.

Another day, we were down at Barking Power Station in the Thames estuary, filming fish. Their return to a cleaner Thames was being ingeniously monitored by observing which species were regularly caught in the power stations' cooling-water filters. The fish didn't always survive the experience, but they weren't wasted. There was a travellers' encampment in waste ground beyond the power station, and some nights the men would come over the fence, filch the whiting from the filter and take them back to cook over the Calor gas stoves in their caravans.

But the most remarkable examples of co-existence were the big domestic rubbish tips east of London, now an almost vanished habitat since rubbish began to be dumped in the North Sea. As warm as compost and seething with food opportunities they were immensely hospitable to all kinds of creatures. Once, I happened to be prospecting a tip in Hackney on the first day of the shooting season, and met a gang of noisy pheasants fleeing in from the east – one of the most cheering things I have seen in London. When we finally chose a tip in Rainham as our location, it was chiefly for its rashes of exotic plants sprung from food refuse and discarded bird seed. The species faithfully recorded Londoners' cosmopolitan appetites. There were water melons, mung beans, cumin and coriander – and thickets of marijuana. But as we were admiring a delicate Mediterranean spice plant, a passing truck driver, with a load of sheeps' intestines in tow, roared angrily at us, 'You ought to tell the truth about this place.' Chastened, we filmed him as he dumped his offal, which was promptly smothered by a white veil of voracious seagulls.

2

Working on *The Unofficial Countryside* gave me a taste for wild corners that had slipped out of the system, and, rather admiring the opportunism of the thornapples and black redstarts, I tried going on impromptu forays myself. Away on Penguin business I would while away evenings in strange towns and spare hours on car journeys following my nose into the wasteland. I haunted the rough ground around northern railway stations, got re-acquainted with the wilder corners of the New Forest, and became too adept for my own safety at scanning road verges whilst I was driving.

Once, with an evening appointment to keep in Edinburgh, I took the sleeper up to Aviemore, hitched a 5 a.m. taxi ride to the old Caledonian pine forest of Abernethy, and walked through the spring dawn to the osprey reserve at Loch Garten. It was like Scotland before the Fall. For three hours I ambled through the birch and Scots pine woods with herds of roe deer only yards in front of me. Crossbills and red squirrels showered nibbled pinecones around me, and I saw my first crested tits, trapezing high up in the canopy. Turning a corner in a track I came face to face with a blustering capercaillie, as big as a turkey. And echoing across Loch Garten I heard the last wintering whooper swans and the trills of the first common sandpipers. When I finally reached the osprey hide, and spent a morning watching these huge piebald raptors haul salmon back to their tree-top nest, it didn't seem inappropriate that it was the humans here who were effectively in cages. By teatime I was in Edinburgh.

When I left Penguin and went freelance (thanks to the sales of *Food For Free*) I was able to be more choosy about my trips. I became a map-worm, browsing over Ordnance

Survey sheets, plotting expeditions, trying to imagine the look and feel of the land behind the formal diagrams. I began to get a feel for certain combinations of bunched contour lines and switchback lanes. I combed the charts for the stipple of remnant heathland, for woods whose edges frayed down narrow valleys as they did round Dartmoor, for mysterious inland 'islands' (like Fritham in the New Forest, and Danbury in Essex) where tracks and hedges seemed to isolate a whole capsule of countryside, for ancient ditches that stretched out long curls of green in an otherwise orderly arable fieldscape. It was a kind of divination, and sometimes I was quite content with the imaginary landscapes I conjured from the map.

The two habitats I'd grown up with, woods and commons, had the strongest spell. Commons – both on the map and in life – were now often no more than ghosts of their former selves, an echo in a name, a soft, fan-like pattern of tracks that were formed when the land was unfenced. But woods were altogether more substantial. The mid-seventies was the time when Oliver Rackham's writings about woodland history were beginning to attract attention. I don't think I had ever given much thought to the origins of woods before: they seemed just to be there. But I was much taken with the idea that many native woods were direct descendants of our natural forest cover, and that they had been ingeniously exploited by humans for at least 4,000 years. Rackham revived the term woodsmanship for this process of conservative use, to distinguish it from the heavy-handed management involved in establishing and running plantations. Woodsmanship relied on the natural ability of our native trees to renew themselves. Coppicing, for example – harvesting wood by cutting trees down to the base every ten years or so – makes use of the fact that most trees regenerate naturally when cut down, provided they have enough light. It is a cyclical, speeded-up version of what happens when a wood is opened out naturally by a gale, say, with whole trees blown down and others snapped off near the ground.

The Knowledge

I loved the idea that ancient woods had special 'indicator plants', species like wood anemone, archangel, oxlip, lily of the valley, which were poor colonizers and grew most happily on sites which had been more or less continuously wooded. Woods crammed with these plants seemed like life rafts. They were social monuments, too. You could often spot them on maps, surviving out on the poorest soils of the parish, their edges following old, wavering boundary lines.

Armed with these clues, I went wood-crawling, sometimes with maps, sometimes just stopping the car at a glimpse of a clump of anemones, a bank and ditch, or just a suggestive fuzziness in the understorey. I was astonished by the variety of what was conventionally lumped together as woodland, and at the ability of natural tree communities to find their own ways of living in every kind of situation. I saw juniper woods on the west coast of Scotland, ash woods growing out of cracked limestone in Yorkshire, and a horizontal wood of prostrate holly and blackthorn on the shingle at Dungeness, first mentioned in Saxon documents. Near the Suffolk coast there was a bluebell wood on pure sand, and a few miles inland at Staverton, a two-storey wood, where rowan and holly had seeded in the crowns of old oak pollards. Cornwall had ancient wind-pruned thickets on the Dizzard cliffs that came up no higher than your chest, and a great oakwood in the Fal estuary that was flooded by the high tides at the spring equinox. I saw it one March, with the river, white from china clay, lapping the low oak branches and first primroses.

There were even places that were both woods and commons, especially in the Chilterns and Sussex Weald, and the Cotswolds, where some were compartmented with ancient walls. In all these places there was evidence of frugal human activity in partnership with the woods, not against them: coppice stools, many hundreds of years old, pollards, where the trees had been harvested at a higher level, saw-pits, wood-hedges, hammer-ponds.

A ten-minute stroll anywhere – up the Top, where I thought I knew every tree by heart, or in an unknown wood next to a lay-by, became a celebration of the variety of woody growth, and its response to sawing, chopping, nibbling, wind, flood and fungus. And my mental woodland map, of lilies of the valley and lime trees stretching from Durham down to the New Forest, began to feel like the chart in Fleur Adcock's effervescent poem *Proposal for a Survey*: 'A map of Poet's England from the air . . . We'll see the favoured regions all lit up – the Thames a fiery vein, Cornwall a glow. Tintagel like an incandescent stud, most of East Anglia sparkling like Heathrow.'

Or rather that was how it felt in those parts of the home country that hadn't had their individuality flattened out by intensive forestry or agriculture. In parts of East Anglia the landscape itself had become little more than a map, a shadow of what it had once been. The field oaks on the ancient boundary banks had been felled, the ditches turned into canals, the fields ploughed up to the very edge of the road. I would spot a wood on a map with an outline as tantalizingly irregular as an amoeba, imagine something whose pedigree was almost as old, and find that in real life it was buried under a pall of conifers. There were no breathing spaces, no margins where things could happen, no white land. Except along the coast and a few islands of ancient wood and heath, the landscape had been stripped down to its skeletal parts, the dead outlines and inventories of an estate survey.

We all have mental charts of the landscape – maps of ownership, work, travel, ambition, loss; literal maps and maps which echo the magical, aboriginal plans of childhood. Often it is nature, with its continuity and profusion and power to evoke associations that forms the link between these imaginings and the landscape itself.

Yet nature has plans of its own, and we cannot expect it always to carry our cultural memories or faithfully conform to our notions of heritage. Rambling around the country with something of the naïve enthusiasm of an eighteenth-century Picturesque traveller eventually led me to see my home patch in a more historically informed light. But this increased the puzzles of the landscape rather than solving them. If there is a history of a landscape, does it also follow that there is a morality of landscape? What part does human activity really have in making the landscape, and what does it do to our sense of nature as property? And what does this close continual contact we have with nature — living and helping to shape an environment for ourselves — tell us about our place in the natural scheme of things?

Away Games

In the mid-eighties I began travelling around Britain not just as a curious tourist, but on journalistic assignments. Most writers are obliged to do some journalism to keep the wolf from the door, even if they don't enjoy it. Luckily I do. I like the challenge of tackling ideas that I would never have thought of myself, of being obliged, for once, to listen to other people's opinions and trust my own first impressions. Sometimes these expeditions begin as purely personal outings, revisiting old haunts, chasing good weather or migrant birds, and only later trigger an idea for a piece of writing. But more often these days a commission sets them off – and sets at least some of the agenda. I am posted to an unfamiliar place, expected to form a brief but meaningful relationship with it and consummate the whole affair in a matter of days. Often it all has to be done in an unseemly haste and with none of the traditional diffidence with which one is supposed to approach places away from home. On assignment I've circumnavigated London in 48 hours, looking at what had happened to my old unofficial countryside sites in the face of the new broom of urban development; stayed in the summer holiday resort of Great Yarmouth in the dead of winter; been disorientated in the vast wastes of the Sutherland Flow Country, trying to put solid form to a landscape which became the centre of the forestry grants scandal in 1987; and stitched together an impressionist portrait of the turbulent fortunes of the Severn estuary from a rag-bag of memories and a lightning tour crammed between hospital visits to a sick relative.

The end products of these fleeting acquaintanceships are, I suspect, sometimes facile and over-personal. Traditional wisdom insists that the countryside is a mystery that can only be understood with patience and from the inside. You must be summered and wintered, work the soil, go through the rites of killing, learn 'the ways' – and your place – before you can be fully admitted. Rural mythology is full of wariness towards the 'offcomer', and the journalistic intruder, often an impractical, emotional townee to boot, is doubly suspect.

But the world has been closing in on parish fastnesses, challenging both their identity and independence, and their claims to a privileged, localized wisdom. Industrial pollution now rains indiscriminately across woods and fields just as farm pesticides seep into urban watercourses. We know that a tree in Ambridge is as integral and important a part of the earth's ecosystem as one in Amazonia. Even the definition of the countryside as a special kind of place is becoming hazy as farming plays a less dominant role and rural populations become more mobile. These changes paradoxically make local distinctiveness even more precious; but they also mean it is a quality which is rooted in places themselves, more than in the perceptions of a particular group of people.

*

Yet exploring that borderland, trying to find common meanings in what is local and special, has always been a preoccupation of country writing. One of my other jobs during the eighties was working on the life of the eighteenth-century clergyman Gilbert White, who was one of the first writers to try to make sense of the closed world of rural life for a wide audience. White is best known as the author of the first (and still the best) book of popular natural history. *The Natural History of Selborne*, published in 1789, helped to shape our national love of the countryside and found the science of ecology. White was also a life-long diarist, with a remarkable sensitivity to place and moment. His journal entries were the raw material for his book, and it is not playing with words to call him a journalist. *Selborne* is composed as a series of letters, a collection of datelined bulletins from 'the green retreats'. It links for the first time, and without any of the patronizing quaintness that characterizes nineteenth-century rural writing, the worlds of nature and the village. It blends poetry and science, the ordinary and the exotic. Earthworms, echoes, the making of rushlights, the mysteries of migration all put in an appearance. And somehow, this farrago of diary jottings, historical asides, full-length monographs and gossip ('I forgot to mention . . .' is one of his favourite phrases) seems able to speak *from* the village at the same time as objectively *about* it. It is a masterpiece of diplomacy as well as natural history.

I came to *Selborne* late in life. When I first tried to read it in my late teens I was put off by its rambling disorder and larding of stiff eighteenth-century prose. When, many years later, a commission to write an introduction obliged me to get under the book's skin, I was astonished that I had ever found it less than bewitching. The more I understood them the more sympathetic I found White's sensibilities. His favourite birds, the swifts and swallows and martins, were admired not just out of scientific curiosity, but because they were 'entertaining' and 'sociable'. He hated the moment when they departed as a melancholy sign that winter was on the way; and was enough of an early Romantic to hope (against all his scrupulous scientific beliefs) that a few slept away the winter somewhere in the parish.

He seemed to be engagingly human too, some way from either a saint or a soulless rationalist. He enjoyed gambling, food, London literary life and Oxford scholarship almost as much as the Selborne countryside. His book was the result of 18 years of fastidious and subtle writing and editing. Yet he has still been claimed as a citizen of that mythical, arcadian world where rural wisdom is – by definition almost – artless, instinctive, homespun. He has been cast and explained away as a recluse, an ascetic, even a kind of primitive. (One modern editor wrote that 'White rejoiced in his world, as a spaniel may rejoice to find new smells in the hedgerow').

Working on his biography involved a fascinating comb through White's papers and correspondence which soon demolished the myth of Parson White, the bumpkin with the gift of words. I followed his tracks through the Selborne countryside, convinced that the local landscape had a direct influence in shaping his perspective on the natural world. His Journals, from which *Selborne* was quarried, repeatedly echo the shape and rhythms of the surrounding countryside. The best are crystal-sharp miniatures which can catch the essence of a moment in a few vivid strokes: '30 Oct 1788. Larches turn yellow: Ash leaves fall; the hanger gets thin.' Or in longer and more sympathetic ponders: '3 April 1791. The chif-chaf . . . is heard in the Hangar & long Lythe. They are usually heard about the 21 March. These birds, no bigger than a man's thumb, fetch an echo out of the hanger at every note.' Many of the entries show an intense concentration of detail, and often work by joining together carefully selected and apparently incongruous images – domestic to exotic, stolid to fugitive, earth to air. On the first day of February, 1785, he noted that 'On this cold day about noon a bat was flying round Gracious street pond, dipping down & sipping the water, like swallows, as it flew: all the while the wind was very sharp, & the boys were standing on the ice!'

I tramped about all these places – Gracious Street, the ponds, the beech-clad Hanger above the village, with its network of sunken paths and banks. I followed White's favourite walks through Dorton Common and the Lythes below the village and tried to make my own functional jottings on the essential character of the landscape: 'Nov 29th. What you see is *foreground*: layered sandstone, tree roots contoured round it, fungus on the dying trees, young saplings in the gaps left when they fall . . . Beyond the woods – tiny copses in further dips, just visible from their bare winter twigs; pools of floodwater, runnels, channels, springs, fenced and hidden by trees, invisible until you come close . . .'

I was secretly glad that White's shade never appeared to answer mundane queries about his height or appearance. But what always seemed present, as an example, was his rapt, intimate attention to the detail of natural life. I felt this especially in the 'hollow lanes', the old sunken road system of the parish. In places these trackways are 15 feet below ground level, and I had the sense of being inside the landscape, not just observing it.

The lanes were formed, as White had graphically put it, 'by the traffic of ages and the fretting of water', and before I knew the parish very well I had taken a conventional heritage view of them. 'The hollow ways', I wrote in a piece in 1980, 'are a geological record of Selborne's history. In the manner of an archaeological dig, the deeper they sank the more they revealed of the parish's experience.' It was a neat idea but too glib by half, and the more I walked the lanes the vaguer these traces of the past seemed to be. What struck me was not their ancient echoes but their insistent roots in the present. In spring they were gaudy with wild flowers, drifts of sweet woodruff, herb paris, wild garlic, red campion and golden saxifrage that seemed to relish these humid, sheltered ravines even more than their native woodland. In high summer they would become fern-draped tunnels, with clouds of insects hanging in the still air and picked out by the dappled light. Sometimes gaps appeared in the hedges where storms had upturned a tree, set off the 'fretting' again and laid open tangles of knotted roots that seemed to defy gravity as well as the weather. They had a grainy, 'historic' feel, but only in a generalized sense that could have meant five or 500 years old.

Antique natural landscapes don't incorporate the past in neat chronological layers. Because they are alive there is a continuity between what they were and what they are. Their past is, in both senses, always present. Trees have annual rings, but their outermost bark is as old as their hearts. Hedges age not by expansion but by ever-increasing internal variety. In the same way, the hollow lanes don't preserve the effects of floods and freeze-ups locked in their proper strata by tenacious trees or ferns. Every so often they are turned inside out. Their history is rhythmic more than linear, just as 'hollowness' is not so much a fixed fact of the landscape round Selborne as a tendency, a cast. People wore out the sunken lanes following what were already natural channels across the land. Tunnels erode under ancient beech roots and are filled up again by landslides. Streams sink into the sandstone rock, choke up with fallen wood and are flushed out again by winter rains. Habit, so to speak, becomes habitat.

I don't think it is a coincidence that White was fascinated by the hollow ways. They symbolized so much of his own outlook, being both highly local and a link with the outside world, anciently rooted and intensely alive. He saw no contradiction in this, or in the fact that, in living systems, permanence and change could co-exist. One of the heartening lessons of *Selborne* for the present is the sense it gives of the landscape's durability. The parish received a terrible pounding from the elements during the 1770s and 1780s – floods, massive hailstorms, landslides, prolonged droughts and freeze-ups, even an earthquake – but still survived. So did Gilbert's faith in the resilience of life.

2

I finished the biography just before Christmas 1985, and began dreaming of the spring even earlier than usual. Saying *au revoir* to a man who had been such close and stimulating company for the past four years was, I guessed, going to leave a large hole in my life. I didn't want to be cooped up indoors as well, pining for the Hanger. Besides, I was harbouring a superstitious and entirely sentimental wish to see the book on its way as the swifts and martins, White's and my favourites, coasted back into the country. It was collar-holding time again.

But the weather, which was already beginning to show signs of its now all too familiar instability, had other plans. February 1986 passed with a prolonged freeze-up that decimated bird populations. March relented a little but closed with a ferocious gale that cut the first serious swathe through the old beech pollards on Berkhamsted Common and ushered in another fortnight of sleet. In mid-April I was on the north Norfolk coast, and the north-easterly wind was so bitter that I had to shelter behind a sea wall to watch the brent geese which still had not started their migration back to Siberia. At the end of the month the wind at last tacked round to the south, and during a brief, balmy spell on the 25th of April, I saw my first lone swallow of the year.

Two days later the nuclear reactor at Chernobyl went up. When the swifts did arrive after their 6,000-mile migration from Africa, they had to fly through a cloud of radioactive dust that already blanketed most of Europe. By May Day the chilling rain had returned, this time full of radioactive caesium, and the government started to issue nervous warnings to people living in the Lake District. On this ancient festival of fertility and new life spring lambs and spring water were declared forbidden fruits.

Those first few days of May were a disquieting, unreal time. The south of England was at minimal risk, yet Chernobyl's fall-out cloud became a terribly physical reminder – the worse for being invisible – of what had previously been just an insubstantial dread. In Eastern Europe it had been drifting across the landscape for two days before they even knew of its existence. I was relieved that I had something else to do and think about. Some while before I had arranged an early May birdwatching trip to Dorset with my old friend and fellow birder from Norfolk days, Peter. Dorset has a famously diverse landscape, and we planned to shuttle across it for three or four days, between seabird cliffs and nightingale copses and what remained of the county's heathland. We hoped we might see some of the migrant birds that had so far (and symbolically, it now seemed) failed to materialize in the home counties. I was also, I must admit, feeling the need to write something about what had happened, something perhaps on what the ill wind seemed like viewed from an ancestral countryside . . . Writer's tic is a chronic and probably incurable affliction, even when one is trying to escape.

When we arrived on the south Dorset coast at Abbotsbury the weather had taken a decided turn for the worse. A fierce wind was blowing cold air (and more Chernobyl dust) in from central Europe, and under the pewter-coloured sky Chesil Bank's seven miles of shingle looked like something the tide had washed in. The Bank walls in the longest string of tidal lagoons in Britain, and we'd been hoping they might have proved an inviting refuge to gale-weary migrants. But the water level was high, and the surface so choppy that even Abbotsbury's famous swans had taken to skulking in the reeds. Only the resident flamingo was wading about in the open water. The few swallows and swifts that were hawking for insects were flitting, heads down, over a mass of miniature breakers. They looked as if they were still on migration, braving the squalls over Biscay, not already here and supposedly making our summer. As the wind began whipping sheets of freezing drizzle into our faces we retreated behind a breakwater, peering occasionally at the buffeted birds more out of a sense of duty than celebration.

It was a miserable way to spend a mid-May afternoon and reminded me uncomfortably of how often I had been frustrated by this county in the past 20 years. Dorset and I have unfinished business. It has always been my soft spot, a landscape of the mind, an idea against which my resistance to idyllic images of the countryside crumbles away. The Dorset of my imagination is a cryptic, ancient landscape, locked behind great bulwarks of chalk and dwarfing the humans that inhabit it. It is always either late March, with rooks tossing over an ash copse, or midsummer on the bare sweeps of Eggardon Hill, with Vaughan Williams's 'Lark Ascending' playing somewhere in the background. I only have to read the village names on the map – Mappowder, Melbury Bubb, Winterbourne Whitchurch, Melcombe, Sydling, Hazelbury Bryan – strung out like old almanack entries along the yellow by-roads, and I am back buried in those 1950s children's television serials that seemed always to be set in south country rectories; or in a scene in Geoffrey Household's *Rogue Male*, where the hero, on the run

from Hitler's agents, goes to ground in the Marshwood
Vale with his adopted cat Asmodeus. (The film of the book
was even more evocative, Peter O'Toole striding up by the
dense hazel hedge while rhapsodic string music played.)

Dorset in the flesh is invariably as compromised and
down-to-earth as this day on Chesil. But I still keep going
back, and every trip becomes an attempt to exorcize my
own fantasy or, just perhaps, find one place where it is true.

*

The next day, Dorset lay under a more tangible veil. The
wind had dropped and a dense fog had come down over the
whole coastal strip. The barrows and Celtic field systems
that stretch from the Winterbournes up to Eggardon and
Toller Porcorum were no more than thickenings in the
mist. Where there should have been ramparts of downland
sweeping up from the trackways, there were thin smid-
geons of over-fertilized grass behind barbed wire fences,
fading into oblivion.

We nosed our way down towards Powerstock Common,
and the gloom lifted a little. In medieval times there had
been a small hunting forest here. More recently much of the
common had been covered by Forestry Commission plantations. Now it had been bought by the county wildlife
trust and the first tentative clearings of the conifer blanket
had begun. The edges of the rides and the compartments
where the plantings had failed were thick with self-sown
oak and birch, and it wasn't hard to see how quickly the
original woodland would reclaim this site if it was given a
chance.

But the air was about as invigorating as waterlogged felt
under the pumice-coloured sky. We tramped between the
rows of spruces, craned our binoculars in every direction,
and caught tantalizing glimpses of a buzzard and a sparrow-
hawk, vanishing behind the trees. Blackcaps gave desultory
bursts of song in the undergrowth, glanced at the weather,
and us, and hunched back into moody silences. It was only

after what seemed like hours of walking that we lighted on one of the last remnants of the original forest – a tract of bony, fern-draped, elfin oaks on low-lying boggy ground. We squelched about among the rushes, relieved at last to see the primroses and marsh marigolds which had been so conspicuously absent on the rest of the common. And at last we heard, and then spotted, our first willow warbler of the year, its tiny olive body, the brightest spot in the half-light, visibly shaking with the sheer force of its song.

And that was how the day went on. We edged further west and roller-coasted in and out of the mist. One moment the whole coastline vanished, the next the hilltops. It was as if we were trapped in some seasonal fable, and being visited by ghosts of Dorset Past and Yet to Come. The chalk country was shorn of wild flowers but we found that Geoffrey Household had been right to hide his hero away in the Marshwood Vale. There was a hidden landscape there with ragged hedges as wide as the lanes, purple orchids on the verges and wild daffodils in the meadows. We saw almost no birds in the open countryside, but were spoilt for them when we arrived at Radipole Lake, slap in the middle of Weymouth's new shopping centre.

Radipole is one of Dorset's better jokes at the expense of the expectant traveller. It was once the estuary of the river Wey, until the building of the Westham bridge dammed off the tidal flow and turned it into a freshwater lake alongside the town's goods sidings. Now it is a Royal Society for the Protection of Birds reserve, but doesn't try to hide its suburban origins. Even the paths through the reedbeds were made from the rubble of Weymouth houses bombed during the war, and are decked out with all kinds of stowaway garden plants through the summer.

Peter and I wandered about the tracks, spent a while in the hides and got the distinct impression that Dorset's missing birds had all decamped down here to the coast. Swifts were dashing about the pools, so low that we could hear the rush of their wings as they shot past our heads. Bearded tits dithered deep in the reedbeds. The whiplash calls of Cetti's warblers rang out against the noise of the ring road traffic.

But this feast of birds made us greedy. At the main hide there was talk of a bee-eater down on Portland Bill. It seemed almost against nature that such a flamboyant Mediterranean bird should have found its way to England on a day like this, even by accident. I have watched bee-eaters in Spain and the Languedoc, dazzling kaleidoscopes of orange and turquoise as they arrow up from the telegraph wires. They conjure up the warm south for me like nothing else, and the merest whisper of them would have set me off, murk or no.

So we drove down to Portland, the rugged promontory at the end of Chesil Beach that Hardy called 'the Gibraltar of Wessex'. The mist had reduced the grim backcloth of quarries and naval bases to a series of monochrome blocks, but when we reached the bird observatory at the tip of the peninsula we were told that, yes, there had been a bee-eater that morning, up near the signalling station. As darkness closed in on us (at about 4 o'clock) the foghorns began to sound, and we drifted on amongst a ghostly landscape of wet radio masts. I can't imagine what a bee-eater, used to nothing more oppressive than a sea-breeze on the Algarve, would have made of it, but we gave up. If Dorset had, that day, been saying something about the presumptuousness of trying to catch its *genius loci* on the wing, so to speak, it had succeeded. As we drove in slow motion towards our hotel along the coast road, I had a flash of sympathy for Hardy's bleak view of humans' fate at the hands of nature, and toyed with beginnings for his unwritten novel on the hapless country writer: 'If a man had stood on the ridge above the Bank and looked towards the sea, his view would have been no more elevated than the cormorant's of the land. Rock, water, ancient barrows all seemed part of a single rayment' . . . For a moment the dour whaleback of Chesil loomed out of the fog on our left, the pebbles as big as oranges . . . 'Yet if he had looked closer he might have glimpsed two figures. They were making sure and quick steps, yet their faces wore expressions of agitation, like messengers that had lost their way.'

On our final morning the fog had gone but the wind was getting up again. We drove down to Poole Harbour and then to Arne – the last remnant of Hardy's Egdon Heath. Both were shorn of birds. We tried to walk east along the cliffs at Kimmeridge, hoping for a glimpse of puffins and guillemots, but were driven back by showers of razor-sharp shales being torn out by the gale and blown upwards into our faces.

The day had an oppressive, charged feel about it. In a pub on the Purbeck Hills above Lulworth and Tyneham military ranges (where the cottages have barrack numbers) we ate lunch nervously amongst a large gang of young men getting determinedly drunk for the Cup Final. Thinking that things couldn't really get much worse we decided on impulse to go down to the Ministry of Defence tank training ranges at Tyneham that were usually open at the weekend. We drove down the switchback road into the valley for a couple of miles, and were suddenly face to face with the Dorset that had eluded us for days. Around us was an extraordinary prospect. The downland scarp was covered with flowering gorse and derelict tanks. Sheep grazed on a medieval field system, picking their way through cowslips and spent shell cases. We followed the paths from Tyneham down to Lulworth Cove, and in some of the shell craters, now full of blackthorn scrub, nightingales were singing into the gale.

It was unsettling, this marriage of military hardware and wildness, and nowhere more so than in the melancholy remains of Tyneham itself, which had been washed and brushed up and generally restored as a classic example of an historic Dorset hamlet – except that nobody lived there. The villagers were moved out to make way for the training range at the height of the last war, with the promise that they would be able to return when it was all over. They left a note pinned on the village door saying: 'Please look after our village while we are away.'

The army have stayed, and argue that their presence may

not have done much for the village but that it has conserved both landscape and wildlife. Many of the locals agree. But support isn't unanimous. In the little museum which has been created in one of the old cottages, the army have provided a visitors' book, which showed that further afield feelings were mixed. Some visitors had written pleas for the village to be resettled. Others found the paradox of military occupation of such a place too offensive to bear.

But for sheer venom nothing in the visitors' book rivalled the comments of those locals who were protesting – often at length – about the recent invasion of 'plastic cottages' on the site. We were mystified about what these might be, until we discovered that they were props for Bill Douglas's forthcoming film on the Tolpuddle Martyrs, who were transported for forming a trade union during the agricultural depression of the 1830s, when much of southern England's marginal farmland 'went back'. Tyneham, isolated first by geography and then by military occupation, was the only place in Dorset that the director felt had the correct rundown nineteenth-century look. It seemed an ironic comment on our muddled sense of 'heritage', and a salutary end to my facile quest to 'discover' Dorset. But I did like the idea of a community visitors' book. Perhaps every parish should have one, where locals and strangers could carry on their perennial debates.

*

Later that year the Council for the Protection of Rural England issued a campaigning postcard of a view uncannily like Tyneham, over the slogan YOUR COUNTRY FIGHT FOR IT NOW. It was a revival of an old wartime propaganda poster, with a shepherd leading his flock down into a village nestling between the downs, and a glimpse of the Channel – the last ditch between us and the Enemy – just beyond. The 1980s version assumed a quite sophisticated updating by the reader, who was expected to know that the threats were now from within – from industry, agribusiness, village developers. Yet it made the same assumption as in wartime: that the country can be identified with its countryside, and that in some way that isn't to do with literal ownership the landscape is 'ours'. As in 1940, there was less agreement about both these ideas than some liked to imagine.

3

In 1987 a Sunday newspaper asked me if I'd be interested in doing a piece on the changing English village, a long-term view, sampled over a period of nine months. I can't say I warmed to the prospect at first. The site had already been chosen – a showpiece settlement in Warwickshire, winner of Best Kept Village awards, but now in a period of transition. The farms were selling up, the school was under threat, and the old cottages being bought up by commuters taking advantage of a new motorway link that passed just half a mile from the village. It was a depressingly familiar story, and I wasn't sure I had any appetite for charting upwardly mobile lifestyles in the Midlands arable belt.

But having never heard of the village before, let alone visited it, I felt I should at least give it a chance. I travelled up on a late winter's day and padded about by myself, nervous of village sensitivities. I wasn't entirely sure why the paper had gone so unerringly for this place, or whether the villagers knew anything about its plans. I was worried, too, about my own stock responses. It is hard not to take a topographic view of a village at first sight, and Newton seemed to me like a reflection of the bland countryside in which it sat. There were two farms fronting onto the village street, and one more which appeared to have been converted into flats. There was a pub, and a duck pond on a patch of green, and one small general store-cum-post office. The structure seemed to be so clearly laid out, with a fifties estate at one end and the executive villas and cottage conversions at the other, that it would have been foolhardy to take it too seriously.

That was about it. There were no small firms, no surgeries or practices, not even those mainstays of the English village, the tea-shop and the antique dealer. The few marked footpaths that wound out from the village were overgrown and barely used. It gave the odd impression of facing away from the surrounding farmland. It couldn't have been more different from the Chilterns, where the landscape dominates life and conversation, and I began to be intrigued by the terms on which this community had made a life in the country.

I agreed to do the piece, and took as much advice as I could. My main contact was Dave Atkin of the North Warwickshire planning department in Tamworth. He had his own views of what was happening to Newton, and the similar transformations which were occurring all over southern England. The regions themselves were changing, and he reckoned the borderline between north and south had now moved some way north of Birmingham. The boundary between town and country was shifting, too, not just from village-edge development, but because it was increasingly a division between working and home life. In Newton Regis it was some time since more than a handful of inhabitants earned their livelihood inside the village. Even 30 years ago the Leicester coalfield had been a more important employer than the local farms. Now villagers travelled to work in a brick works five miles away, or to small industries in Tamworth. The crunch year for the village had been 1986, when the first section of the Birmingham–Nottingham motorway was opened less than half a mile from the village. Newton suddenly became a short, fast drive from the whole expanding nexus of Midlands enterprise: Wolverhampton, Warwick, Stratford, the National Exhibition Centre, Birmingham Airport. The resulting inflow of commuters might have led to a rash of new high-price housing, but for the fact that the ancient core of the village had been designated a conservation area, and the whole of the parish a minimum-growth zone in the structure plan. But housing, consequently, was at a premium, which meant the under-mining of one of the cornerstones of village mythology – the sense of family lineages inhabiting the same parish, and sometimes the same house, for generations. Dave Atkin told me of other long-running threats to the old order: the opening of a commercial clay pigeon range and the closing of the village school.

But there was one oddity in this story of seemingly re-lentless modernization. Newton was – at least in terms of real estate – still a manorial village. Both the farms, several of the houses, the school and much of the land were owned by the Inge-Innes-Lillingstons, who lived at Thorpe, just north of the village.

As I was going to leave Dave mapped out a route to the village that would give me the best picture of the surround-ing landscape. 'I call it the spire country,' he beamed, the planner vanishing for a moment behind the more familiar English figure of the village enthusiast.

*

Driving up to Newton again later that winter, I could see what he meant. All round Newton the skyline is punctured by church spires. They soar up from Appleby, Orton-on-the-Hill, Seckington, Thorpe, smudged with soot from the Black Country factories to the west, and standing out against a gently swelling, wide open landscape that re-minded me of Suffolk. In Newton itself the church, looking a little the worse for wear and swathed in scaffolding, soared above a cluster of allotments, cottages and school buildings.

I had an appointment in the Queen's Head, which by one o'clock was full of customers, many from outside the vil-lage. The landlord, Ron Starr, is a slight man in his sixties, with a quiet, mischievous energy. He had come here from a roadhouse just outside Tamworth 16 years before. It was meant to be a partial retirement, a busman's holiday in 'a pub in the country'. Now, with two bars and masses of passing trade, he is busier than he ever was in the town. Ron took me on a quick tour of the pub, down to see his spick and span cellar and the letters of commendation from the brewery, and outside to see his 'chimney garden' which was slowly taking shape at the back of the pub. The whole thing had been a last-minute scheme, he told me, beginning with 'the fastest potato harvest known to man. I had them in one week, out the next, and the whole plot sown with chimneys by the end of the month'. His collection of pots and pipes, stuffed with bulbs and geraniums, had the sur-real look of an unfinished sculpture park as they waited for the sun to bring them to life. Many of the pieces had come from the local brick works, donated by friends and custom-ers.

In the bar there were more signs of informal barter. Eggs were going one way, seedlings the other. One disabled man who had to make regular trips to hospital was using the pub as the pick-up point for his lift. Chatting with the regulars I asked what the public services were like. Were the newly deregulated buses reliable? Did the fact that the nearest medical practice (at Polesworth) was three miles away cause any problems? No one seemed to know. The question didn't seem to have arisen. There was no shortage of cars in the village, and those few inhabitants who didn't drive never had a problem getting lifts. Was it different in other places?

Newton, I soon discovered, was a prime example of how the car has stretched the village as well as emptying it. There were the usual bingo evenings and pub quiz leagues held locally, but the villagers' sense of where they *lived*, rather than just resided, wasn't limited by the parish boun-daries. They did their chores, went shopping, got their entertainment in a larger catchment area, that they saw as a kind of extended village. Although the days when goods and services were delivered to the door were missed here, as everywhere, no one I talked to regarded the lack of facilities on the doorstep as seriously reducing the quality of their lives.

Over the street from the pub, Jack Rutherford, one-time farm worker and Chairman of the Parish Council, expressed stout approval of this self-help philosophy. Jack, a widower and no longer very mobile, has lived in the village much of his life, most of it in this dark Grade III cottage. '*They* tell me I must preserve the roof. But can I get *them* to pay for it . . .?' He makes no secret of his strict Tory view of village fortunes. Newton, he believed, was a *good* village. The Lillingstons looked after the fabric and the villagers looked after themselves. The local playing field and pavilion were good examples of the fruits of such partnership. The Lillingstons had donated the land, the Parish Council had levied a penny rate to raise funds for building. Much of the work had been done by the villagers, and one of the farms had lent a tractor for the mowing. Charity, hard work, service, paying your dues – these were what had made the village survive and prosper. He thinks well of the newcomers, and there is no hostility in his nickname of 021s for Brummies (after the city's STD code). They join in. They take his dog for walks. He just wishes that they would be a little less pushy in their efforts to keep the village school open, and would make their children sandwiches for lunch instead of relying on school-dinner handouts. But he is sure that no one in the village wants any new developments, either of housing or light industry and certainly none of the suburban frippery of restaurants and shops. These were the things people moved to Newton to get away from.

Talk of work puts him in a wistful mood. 'There were three tailors in the village once, just to serve the Big House. All that livery!' His house is crammed with family and village mementoes, kept close to hand to save his legs. He showed me a rushlight holder, his late wife's books on herbalism, a pint barrel his father had used to take beer into the fields, reminders of a more spartan life. But it wasn't the working village he missed so much as that immemorial, well-oiled hierarchy of duties and responsibilities he believed were still hanging on by a thread in Newton. Then

108

he fishes out his *coup de grâce*, a glimpse of Jack the Lad: a photo showing him, younger and more worldly, shaking hands with a local Labour politician.

But it wasn't the village's own radical representative. Surprisingly, perhaps, for such an upwardly-mobile community, Newton and its neighbour, No Mans Heath, had elected a Labour member to the Borough Council. Steve Norman is a sales rep for an industrial plastics firm, and lives in a cottage buried deep among the fields and plantations on the northern edge of the parish. He agreed with Jack Rutherford's view of a harmonious village, but laughed at Jack's appropriation of this for his own political side. It is one of Labour's periodic weeks of self-immolation, and he is careful what he says. He sees no real party issues here. There is some unemployment in the area, but it is not a village problem. The lack of cheap housing may become one, but at present there are only five names on the waiting list for council houses, and the conflict between old and new villagers – which was partly a class conflict – was barely noticeable.

What concerned people here was more parochial, he reckoned. The provision of street lights, winning the Best Kept Village award, keeping the school open, and now, above all, the looming threat of the gun club. An outsider from Uttoxeter, who owned a parcel of land on the edge of the village, had applied for permission to open a commercial clay pigeon range. Free enterprise had, for once, confronted the new rural culture's other aspirations, for peace, privacy and security and hadn't stood a chance. Nothing had so completely united the village, from council house to mansion, since the threat to the school.

From their different standpoints both Jack and Steve nominated the new rector, Stan Marriott, as one of the important unifying influences on the village. Stan, in his early sixties, had only been in the parish for 18 months, but had already earned himself the affectionate nickname of the White Tornado, for his energy in getting things done. He and his wife Joan came here from a nearby mining village.

They were convinced that the mutual caring that is evident here is a common and necessary trait in this part of the Midlands, and that it had survived the transition from rural and industrial village to commuter settlement. Stan is a generous and respected man, with a huge sense of humour that has already helped him to minister to those dark moments that afflict all small communities. He told me how last year an uncanny series of tragedies had struck every member of the bell-ringing team, and that what had helped begin the healing process was a blackly comic hearse race to the cemetery.

He filled in more details of the crisis that had recently faced the village school, when the roll fell into the low twenties and closure had seemed imminent. The village had rallied round and campaigned to save it. But what clinched the outcome was an influx of travellers' children from the permanent site at Alvecote, a few miles west of the village. The roll rose above 40, and the school looked safe – for the time being anyway.

Stan regards the travellers as part of his parish, and visits them regularly. He believes their children have integrated well with local youngsters. He is more concerned about the fate of children generally in the area. They haven't the same mobility as adults, and the image of a carefree country childhood is now a dangerous delusion. The recent spate of child murders in the Midlands had given grim confirmation to what most parents have begun to take for granted – that children are no longer safe playing by themselves in woods and fields. 'They have changed people's perception of country life,' Stan acknowledges philosophically. Now when he is visiting parishioners in the evenings he always phones first, and agrees a coded number of rings on the doorbell.

*

Spring in Newton arrives more conspicuously in the village than in the countryside beyond. Ron Starr's chimneys begin to bloom and stir hopes that Newton might scoop the Best Kept Village award for a third time. There are signs of a new broom in the village store, where Rob Hilditch, a re-dundant welder, and his wife Linda are taking over the re-ins and have plans for extending its stocks and services. The first broods of ducklings from the pond are beginning to make mad forays across the street into the yard of Manor Farm.

This is the larger of the two farms and the tenancy has been in the Wilson family for generations. It is a medium-sized unit of 400 acres on good soil, with a mixture of graz-ing, cereal and potatoes. The current tenant, Stewart Wil-son, a single man in his late thirties, sees no problem in jug-gling the proportions of crops to meet any changes in Common Agricultural Policy quotas for milk or cereal. Nor does he think the current talk of taking farmland out of pro-duction will drive him into trying fashionable crops like flax or evening primrose, or into Pick-Your-Own. Mind you, there was a time when the farm was host to all manner of visitors. Up until a few years ago they had an annual sum-mer dance and barbecue for 1,500 people, twice the number that lived in the village. There are, as yet, no signs of the 'Shire Wars' disturbances that have been disrupting other rural areas, but gatherings of that size were out of the question now. Instead Stewart is looking forward to host-ing a more modest gathering of the breed society for his new French dairy cattle. The only problem he can see in the future is that there is no obvious successor to take over the farm after him.

The problem of succession is more critical at the smaller of the two holdings, Newton Farm. Clifford and Nancy Rowe are nearing retirement and there is no one in the family to carry on the work. They will have to leave the farm when the time comes, and perhaps the village too, with house prices being what they are. As for the farm itself, there is a real chance of it going the way of Old Hall Farm, with the land being broken up and sold off, and the farm buildings converted into dwelling units.

But for the moment, life goes on. It is late in the lambing season, and I walk across the yard with Cliff and his part-time stockman to a pen where a ewe is having a difficult delivery. There is no vet present, but Cliff is accustomed to this kind of situation. He buries his arm deep inside the ewe, and after minutes of intense straining and twisting, pulls out the lamb, feet first. It looks dead to me, but Cliff wipes it down, whirls it round, shakes it like a wet blanket, and suddenly, as if it had been given an electric shock, it jerks into life. A short while later it is nosing blearily towards its mother's teats. Newton Street, locked in mid-morning quiet just a few yards away, and the flat fields beyond, stretching out towards the M42, seem part of another world.

*

14th May, Rogation Sunday. Jack Rutherford has success-fully lobbied for the revival of the ceremony of Beating the Bounds, and at 2.30 p.m. in the afternoon about 50 of us gather by the lych gate of St Mary's Church to circumnavi-gate the parish. The plan is to be back in time for tea. In Selborne, I recall, it used to take three whole days to parade around just 18 miles of boundary.

The weather is ominous for a ceremony that began as a pagan fertility rite before being Christianized in the fifth century. The Chilterns were being lashed by thunder-storms when I left, and up here a sickly haze hangs over the whole landscape. Steve Norman has wisely donned his Pennine walking boots, but most of the company's clothes would be more appropriate for a stroll down to the Queen's Head. Our guide is Bill Tunnicliff, retired hedger and woodman and walking archive. He leads us out of the vil-lage at a furious pace, treating anyone who can keep up with him to a continuous commentary.

It's a pleasant, garrulous assembly, of all ages and from all sections of the village. For many of them this is the first time they have ever explored Newton's home countryside.

The problem is that much of the old field pattern – and the parish bounds it incorporated – has vanished. The old hedges have been grubbed up, and footpaths obliterated by cereal crops on which the sour-sweet smell of pesticide still hangs. We pick our way – straggling already – along trackways that as often as not come to a dead end in an unnavigable drainage ditch. Some of the children fall, with relish, into the mud. Bill cuts his hand climbing over a new fence, but does his best to make sense of this transfigured landscape. He waves towards where the bounds had once been (or perhaps still are, if only we could reach them) and intones the old field names: 'Old Moor, Sandy Spinney, The Common. C'mon.' He has rehearsed his jokes well.

Every so often, in correct Rogation style, we stop for a hymn and a prayer. Gina Cooke, in a red outfit that is the brightest thing in the landscape, plays guitar for the children to sing:

> *The tall trees in the greenwood, the meadows for our play*
> *The rushes by the water, to gather every day.*

Alas, there is not much greenwood left in Newton, and no flowery meadows for playing or picking. For a brief, ungracious moment I feel disgruntled with this village for being so content with its bland, fenced-off countryside, and pine for the Chilterns. I could imagine what the beechwoods would be like in this tempestuous weather – turned into rainforests, full of flayed, whirling leaves, and green mists rising off the bluebells . . .

Just before we reach the old sewage works, the haze turns the colour of fading oil-seed rape. Jack Rutherford, driven here by a friend, peers from a field gate like a soothsayer. 'God's sun shines on the righteous,' he proclaims. 'What does that make us Jack?' a voice shouts back. I recall what the seventeenth-century parson George Herbert had written about the virtues of the Perambulation. It promoted 'Charitie, in living walking and neighbourly accompanying one another, with reconciling differences, if there by any . . .' Around me, this is exactly what people are doing. Newton isn't a village of walkers, and this isn't walking countryside. What occupies them is not their surroundings but 'neighbourly accompanying' – chatting about gardens and holidays and what the children are doing at school. Telling stories, too: 'We had a day out in London. On a coach. Only it broke down and we had to get a bus. Well, everybody was asking everybody else how they felt and would they be worried back at home, when the conductor comes round. Good Lord, he says, what's the matter? Nobody's talked on this route since the war.'

I hear, too, one of Newton's best tales, that so perfectly catches the prevailing mixed feelings about the outsider that it almost amounts to a fable. Not long after Newton had been chosen as the Best Kept Village in north Warwickshire a car drew up outside one of the sixteenth-century cottages on the main street, and a family got out to take a photograph. There was nothing odd about this. The cottage, thatched and timber-framed and tucked up next to the duck pond amidst billowing foxglove borders, is one of the village showpieces. But this family, more venturesome than most, came right over the fence and into the garden, and – to the amazement of the occupiers, watching from inside – posed against the climbing roses. Then, changing their minds, they went back to the car, rummaged about in the boot and returned with a spade. They posed again, this time with the spade firmly planted in one of the beds. The snap was taken, and the satisfied family drove off with their instant, monogrammed comic postcard.

My brief fit of pique is soon banished by the general high spirits and I join in the gossip. I meet a couple who had to leave Newton after the birth of their first child, for a bigger but more economical house in Tamworth, but who are so fond of the village that they come back for a day out whenever they can. The Smedleys moved the other way, decamping to Newton to raise their family. Their children are with them, enjoying the stroll but more intent on collecting snails than noting landmarks. Caroline Smedley is a leading light in the WI, and doing research on parish history (a sparse field, she admits, once you have gone beyond living memory) and Michael is director of a fine art firm in Lichfield, ten miles to the west. They are all deeply fond of the village and would not have it any different. They recognize that it is liable to lose a whole generation from lack of moderately priced housing, but point out that this happens anyway to 20-year-olds in most communities. Michael, especially, enjoys the sense of refuge the village provides when he comes home from work. There was no local protest when the M42 was built, and most Newtonians regard it as a blessing – an easy route out to work and urban pleasures, and an even more welcome lifeline back to family and home, *village* pleasures.

Remarkably, we are straggling back along the outskirts of the recreation ground as teatime approaches, our abbreviated circuit complete. Stan Marriott's peroration near a little covert called Newton Gorse is a masterpiece, as much Bunyan as Herbert. He stretches his arms wide and asks for blessings on an immense cornucopia of living things that might just possibly be within their compass: rabbits, squirrels, oak trees, cuckoos, the staff of life . . . a vision of a vague but encircling green fulsomeness that I suspect exactly catches the way Newtonians feel about their parish.

*

A few weeks later I travelled back to Warwickshire to talk to George Lillingston, whose seat, Thorpe Hall, is a couple of miles north-west of Newton. It was real spring weather at last, and swarms of house martins were busy at the nests around the Hall. For a while I was lost in the labyrinth of outbuildings and estate offices, but we eventually found each other, and settled in the drawing room and I passed on my concern about the state of the local footpaths. He agreed there was a problem. The local network wasn't as comprehensive or as diligently maintained as it might be. On the other hand he hadn't noticed much local pressure for access – particularly along those paths that originated as field-workers' short cuts. Perhaps people up here were more reconciled to agriculture leading the way than they were in the more environmentally anxious south? It wasn't, I could see from his wry smile, an entirely rhetorical question.

He was well aware of what lay behind some of my queries, and rejected any suggestion that Newton's air of placidity results in part from being under a benevolent squirearchy. 'It would be hard enough being any kind of interventionist squire in the 1980s, even if I lived in the village. Three miles away – *and* in a different county – it's downright impossible.'

But he did lay a modest claim to having set in motion the transformation of the village that led to its present social mix. We had moved into a quiet room at the centre of Thorpe Hall, away from the din of the estate lawnmowers. 'When I came here in the 1950s, Newton was still a Victorian village. There were one-up, one-down cottages with outside lavatories. It needed a boost to its self-respect, an injection of new blood with aspirations for themselves and the village. So we built four semi-detached three-up, three-down cottages in Hames Lane, and then demolished Newton House Farm – an ugly place that spoilt the view of the church – to make room for bungalows.'

He toyed with the phrase 'social engineering' to describe what he did, but it sounds too harsh and grandiose for a scheme which, after all, simply reflected the mood of the times. He was well aware that the lack of first-time housing was likely to cause problems in the future, and said that he was already examining the viability of housing association schemes.

*

Summer comes, a few well-loved names enter the Register of Deaths, and a Mr Present Lee joins the list of marriage witnesses after a particularly high-spirited travellers' wedding. I heard no scurrilous or even mildly hostile tales about the travellers during my whole six months of visiting Newton. The village is fond of storytelling, but seems to have little use for outright gossip. There are occasional good-humoured nudges about certain individuals' fondness for the bottle, but nothing scandalous or unkind. Into this vacuum pour the mischievous spoofs invented by Bob Lane. Bob leads a packed life as a garage owner, folk music enthusiast, parish councillor, smallholder and general entrepreneur. He also runs the only bed-and-breakfast establishment in the village, in the commodious setting of Newton House, and every so often starts a rumour about an impending 'change of use'. It has been destined to become the venue for an open-air rock festival, the headquarters of an extreme religious sect and a dubious foreign consulate. The village, for its part, pretends to believe these tales, as if it needs a continuing shadowy threat from outside, however improbable.

But on those topics that preoccupy village watchers – housing and employment especially – Newtonians are largely silent, even unconcerned. John Bird runs a community work programme in Tamworth, where there are currently 3,600 unemployed and only 80 job vacancies. But he believes the problem is less pressing in the countryside. There is more scope in a village economy for multiple employment, do-it-yourself, part-time work. He took me to see his greenhouse where he had built a brilliant device for providing controlled watering, converted from a flushing lavatory cistern.

It is a kind of ingenuity that is echoed throughout the village. A pair of young men have set themselves up with a chain-saw as a mobile logging team. The man who is repainting the Queen's Head doubles as a carpet layer. Rob and Linda Hilditch have already expanded their business at the village store to provide a video loan service and an off-licence. They are currently working 18 hours a day. Rob sorts the mail first thing, runs the shop in the daytime and fits in deliveries to pensioners whenever he can find a spare moment. Linda drives to market for supplies before going off to her second job as a computer operator. It is way past 6 o'clock on a Friday evening, and customers are still popping into the shop for bottles of shampoo, soft-drinks (quaffed on the spot), a couple of onions, bits and pieces overlooked in the weekend shopping. Rob and Linda have noticed a pattern in the villagers' buying habits. People from the council estate spend more, on better quality goods, west-end Newtonians use the shop for things they have forgotten to buy in the town. The Hilditches are grateful for their custom, but hope everyone realizes that village shop economics are always precarious and that if the shop goes so will the Post Office.

*

The next day, Flower Festival Saturday, is mercifully bathed in sunshine. Newton's countryside looks as green and bosky as anywhere in England on a fine June day, and inside the village the farm tractors have been out tidying up the verges until the street is as smartly shorn as a municipal park. Bill Tunnicliff has heard a rumour that Newton is favourite to walk off with the Best Kept Village award again, and is fretting over some barely visible weeds in the graveyard grass. I tease him that if I was a judge I would disqualify the entire village for over-fussiness.

But it is hard not to be wooed by the displays in the church. This year the theme is country crafts, and the stands are decorated with mixtures of flowers and hand-made goods. Some are modern – loaves, lacework, home-made wine; some are mementoes, and one of the displays is set off against a 1919 peace celebration tablecloth, washed spotless for the occasion. Way above us hangs another odd conjunction: one of the church bells carries a seventeenth-century inscription written backwards, to ward off evil spirits. I sit chatting with the village women, with swallows dipping in and out of the church porch, and realize that Newton is getting pleasantly under my skin. One young woman is here to visit her parents for the weekend and confesses that, like me, she prefers wild country, and moved to the Dales to escape Newton's 'claustrophobia'. But I am

118

beginning to understand what keeps the rest here. It hasn't much to do with the usual preconceptions of village life. Newton isn't rustic or quaint or arty. It has more or less divorced itself from agriculture, from fossilized notions of 'heritage', even from its own landscape. And though it is too prosperous to be typical in this respect, it has given robust answers to the conventional belief that villages automatically decline when they become non-working dormitories or are missing a generation. Most Newtonians want something more limited but quite specific from their village. It is an oasis, a bubble in the green, a home base, a hybernaculum, and the villagers regard their neighbours as their chief amenity. There are plenty of natural models for using the environment as a protection rather than a resource; but given the importance of the church in what must, like the rest of England, be at heart a secular community, perhaps it would be simpler to see this village to a place of sanctuary.

4

What came to be known as the Battle of the Bogs in 1987 was a border conflict with an almost Byzantine complexity of layers. At its heart was the Flow Country, 1,500 square miles of wild peatland in Caithness and Sutherland, home to tens of thousands of wading birds and a scattered community of crofters. Ranged against them were the forces of commercial forestry, attracted here, as to many upland areas, by the expectation of cheap and apparently useless land, and hoping to create what would be the biggest single forestry estate in Britain.

It was the latest chapter in a familiar and long-simmering squabble about afforestation. But the Flow Country had provided some extra and highly combustible ingredients. Distinguished conservationists were arguing that it was a wilderness of international importance, on a par with Serengeti and Amazonia, and there were counter charges from landed Scottish interests that the whole landscape was 'a foul, bankrupt land . . . a denuded wilderness through man's intrusion'. There were accusations of absentee land-lordism and bureaucratic English meddling in Scottish affairs, whiffs of tax-avoidance loopholes and dreams of a job bonanza. When the press discovered that there were celebrities involved as well, that show business figures such as Terry Wogan and Cliff Richard owned blocks of 'in-vestment forest' in the Flows, the argument became a hotly debated national issue.

It was a bemusing confrontation, on a scale more usual in land feuds a continent or two away than in our small and already intensively settled islands. But to some onlookers (and some of the participants) the Flows *were* as foreign as Brazil or Antarctica, a sodden, midge-infested quagmire whose cultural and biological values were mystifying.

When I flew up in late July to cover the story, it was un-known territory for me, too, the furthest north I had been in the British Isles, and I wondered if it overcome a long-standing distaste for bleak uplands. I was based in Golspie, a pleasant little golfing and fishing resort on the east coast. It was full of cafés, boutiques and estate agents, and when I explored it on my first evening, with the swifts racing be-tween the chic cottage conversions, it was hard to believe that this was the gateway to an expanse of primeval bogland the size of Lancashire.

Yet the region was no stranger to land battles. On a ridge overlooking the town is a statue of the first Duke of Suther-land, clad in an imperious red sandstone robe. Early in the last century the English-born Duke had been responsible for the notorious Sutherland Clearances. Between 1814 and 1820 he evicted a third of the entire population of the county from their homes (by burning them down in most cases) to make way for sheep ranching and shooting, and to provide cheap labour for his factories on the coast.

His agent's defence of the purge has an ironic ring in the current circumstances. Their intention, he said, was 'to render this mountainous district contributory as far as possible to the general wealth and industry of the country, and in the manner most suitable to its situation and peculiar circumstances.' The Clearances are an ineradicable part of Highland folk memory, a symbol of all misappropriations of the land, and it was a measure of how deep feelings were running here that each side was accusing the other of initiating 'the New Clearances'.

I went back to my hotel and tried to make some sense of the tangled history of the affair. There did at least seem to be a ground base of scientific facts. What was at stake was the world's largest remaining concentration of blanket bog, a series of rain-drenched plateaux and pools with one of the richest collections of breeding birds in Europe: waders like greenshank, dunlin, golden plover; loch haunters like red-throated divers – birds whose survival depended on expanses of remote, wet wasteland.

'Blanket bog' is a remarkable enough thing in itself. It is a living skin of sphagnum mosses, a vast, intricate carpet of plants, unrooted except for their own mutual entanglements. Sphagnum is honeycombed with capillary tubes and twice as absorbent as cotton wool. In the very high rainfall of the region it becomes permanently waterlogged and swells sufficiently to blanket areas of moss that are dying back. This moribund sphagnum becomes part of the underlying layers of peat, and both live and dead moss form a permanently moist ground base for other plants.

Yet the Flows has never been an uninhabited wilderness. For thousands of years it has also been the habitat of marginal farmers, who have grazed cattle, cut peat on the bogs, and raised crops in the valleys in ways that are entirely compatible with the bird life. Since the Clearances they have borne the brunt of land-use changes.

Trees, until recently, played no significant part in the crofting life. The unrelenting winds and high rainfall made it all but impossible to grow them, except in sheltered valleys. The Forestry Commission, as a result, was a late-comer to the region, and most private forestry companies would not touch it. But in 1979 the Perth-based Fountain

Forestry noticed a happy coincidence of business opportunity and technological know-how. Land prices were low
(as little as £100 a hectare in some places), government
planting grants were favourable, and machines were at last
available that could work in even the most intractable bogs.
Fountain began buying up estates in the Flows and selling
them off to investors (mostly southerners: 72 of the 76
listed in the Scottish land register that year had English
addresses). By the beginning of 1987 it had acquired 40,000
hectares and had earned its investors more than £12 million
in grants and tax exemptions.

Fountain's expansion into the Flows coincided with an
upsurge of interest in the cultural and biological interest of
so-called wastelands. Since the early eighties, the Nature
Conservancy Council (NCC) and the Royal Society for the
Protection of Birds (RSPB) had been noticing drastic
changes in the ecology of the afforested areas of the peatland, whose most conspicuous effect was a plunge in the
breeding populations of wading birds. The NCC, as the
government's statutory advisers on conservation, obtained
an agreement that from February 1987, the Forestry Commission must refer all requests for planting grants in the
Flows to the NCC.

Things had come to a head a couple of weeks before my
trip, when the NCC published a report giving its scientific
evidence on the threat to bird life, and making a plea for a
moratorium on further planting over all the remaining
400,000 hectares of peatland. The report was met with
almost universal hostility from the Scottish establishment.
The Highlands and Islands Development Board said that it
had been drawn up 'without consultation or regard for the
delicate economic and social fabric of the northern Highlands'; Robert McClennan, the SDP MP for Caithness and
Sutherland, had described its scientific conclusions as 'preposterous' and predicted its proposals would lead to the loss
of '2,000 jobs in the long term'.

The forestry lobby accused the conservationists of valu-
ing birds above people and of meddling in affairs beyond its

remit. The conservationists retorted that it was not them but the alien conifers that were driving out – at public expense – both indigenous crofters and new tourists. Each side (it is the shadow of the Clearances again) has accused the other of 'sterilizing' the Flows, showing, to anyone who needed convincing, what a flexible and subjective concept 'productivity' is when it comes to land.

It was not just the scale and venom of the quarrel that were exceptional. Beyond the revelation of show business stars' investment portfolios and the intricacies of government forestry policy, it was stirring ancient and unresolved questions about what we value land for. Was economic usefulness the only indicator? Did wasteland invariably mean wasted land? How could its value as a global asset be compared with its worth as a national raw material?

Later that evening there was music in the hotel bar. It was advertised as a Ceilidh, but it was really a local talent contest for the tourists, an anodyne mixture of country and western and Kenneth McKellar. I recalled another musically tinged evening years before in Fort William, the frontier town between Highlands and Lowlands. That night I had watched two pipers in full regalia sitting in the corner of a bar, playing laments whilst tears rolled down their cheeks, and their wives, done up in stilettos and blue-rinsed hair, sipping gin by their side.

The Flows felt like frontier country too, and with all the feuds, prospectors and bounty hunters it didn't seem too extravagant to view the galloping advance of 'the forestry' as a Great Timber Rush.

*

Next day I drove out into the Flow Country with my guide, Lesley Crenna, local officer for the NCC. Two features of the unplanted peat strike you when you drive in from the hillier land to the south. One is the sense of immense space, of a gently undulating flatness in which there are no straight lines, no harsh colours and, unless you looked for them, very few foregrounds. In clear weather you can often see the peaks of Sky Fea and Genie Fea in the Orkneys, 40 miles to the north.

The other is what I can only describe as a kind of plasticity. The swell of the peat hummocks, the honey-coloured tussocks of sedge, the dark pools all seem, if you stared at them long enough, actually to be moving. Perhaps they are. The whole system is full of mobile water, which regularly seems to overload the sphagnum 'sponge' and spill out to form pools – the dubh lochans. There are many thousands of these, ranged in places like ladders, elsewhere in concentric arcs. From above they have the look of pool clusters on a saltmarsh at low tide, or the pitting in limestone rocks. Against this curving, tremulous landscape the severe stripes and rectilinear furrows of the new plantings seemed misplaced and bizarre enough to have been created by extraterrestrials.

The Flows are really a kind of tundra. During the short, intense sub-arctic summers they buzz with life, with myriads of insects and wading birds. 4,000 pairs of dunlin (35 percent of the European population) nest close to the pools, where they winkle out insects with their toothpick bills. So do the same number of golden plovers, and smaller numbers of greenshank, sandpipers and snipe. There are huge populations of meadow pipits and skylarks and, feeding on these and the abundant voles, are hen harriers and merlin, and peregrines and eagles hunting out of the high ground adjacent to the bog.

I talked to Roy Dennis, director of RSPB operations in the Highlands and a crofter himself, and he admitted that the richness of the birdlife is only just being appreciated, after years of survey work. It might have saved a good deal of misunderstanding if this information had been available earlier, but the remoteness and sheer extent of the land had made surveying a slow, laborious business, and no match for the speed of the new machines. Roy pointed at a map on the wall and said wistfully: 'The land is so flat you could start a bulldozer in Wick and drive it straight to Bettyhill.'

And that, more or less, is what had happened. Out of 65,000 hectares owned by Fountain and the Forestry Commission, roughly half had already been drilled into order with a gusto that would have done credit to the seventeenth-century Dutch fen drainers. Giant excavators had dragged out drainage ditches in the peat, eight feet deep in places, and raised cultivation ridges for the rows of spruce and lodgepole pine seedlings. There were aerial spraying programmes of fertilizer and pesticide, and hundreds of miles of deer fencing had been strung across the moors. Extraction roads had been built whose width was often double that of the local highways.

But as the trade association Timber Growers UK assured me, there was a plan behind it all. The original intention was to create an integrated forest, big enough to be economically self-sustaining and to support at least two new sawmills. One of the keys was the Lairg-Wick-Thurso railway. The new plantations had been sited as close as possible to this line, to minimize transport costs when felling came round. This, TGUK stressed, was why the industry was so anxious to continue its planting programme up to the original target of about 100,000 hectares. Only then could the planned economies of scale be realized.

Looking at the map I could see some logic in this. The railway meandered past many of the plantations – the older blocks round Loch Shin; Strathy Forest, where a sizeable chunk of a National Nature Reserve had been accidentally ploughed up; Wogan's woods near Broubster. But the line was economically precarious, the sawmills still a figment of an economist's imagination, and the whole enterprise looked less like an unfolding plan than an exercise in opportunism.

Even scientific fact had come to be regarded as negotiable currency up here. The most frequent demand I heard from Scottish authorities was for a 'court of appeal' against the hated, English-based NCC. Not just against its proposals (which are only recommendations) but against its evidence, which it was felt should be open to compromise. It was a relief that nobody had any illusions about ecology being an exact science, but disturbing that the age of a tree, say, or the nesting territory of a bird should be regarded as open to something like plea bargaining.

The debate about bird populations was rife with such nimble legalistic footwork. It was still being argued, for example, that plantations *increased* the number and diversity of breeding birds – which, of course, they do, though only of those species that are abundant in woods and gardens throughout Britain, and, temporarily, a few birds of prey. The specialist birds of the wet peatland are completely unable to adapt. But, the foresters argued, surely they could be more sociable, 'bunch up a bit' in the gaps between the new plantations. As Michael Ashmole, Director of Fountain, said of the greenshank, the Flows' third commonest but still somewhat expansive wader: 'If a bird cannot survive on 650 acres, then it doesn't bloody well deserve to survive.'

A decade of intensive research had shown that the greenshanks do try to bunch up for a year or so. Then the stresses of competition and over-population start to show. The birds lose weight, lay sterile eggs, lose chicks by drowning in the drainage ditches or to crows patrolling out of the new plantations, and the inexorable decline into local extinction begins.

Just as serious was the persistence of the argument that commercial forestry was simply restoring a landscape destroyed by earlier farmers. Although some of the region's prehistory is still obscure, fossil pollen and stump fragments show that the last time native woodland (chiefly birch, rowan, hazel and Scots pine) grew on the open plateaux was 4,000 years ago. A decisive wettening of the climate after that meant that young tree growth could not compete with the expansion of the moss on the peat, and woodland survived only in the better drained valleys.

This is not to say that there hasn't been some glamorization of history on the conservationist side. Lesley

Crenna, a Highlander herself, told me that many locals were distressed to hear their homeland repeatedly described as 'the last wilderness' and compared with the Russian Steppes or Alaska. Up here this wasn't seen as a compliment, but as an insult to the work they and their ancestors had put into the land. It made them feel 'like savages'. Sometimes, Lesley told me, crofters burned off patches of the grass – not because it made much difference to the grazing, but to say 'I live here too'.

Even remote corners of the Flows showed the marks of hard, subsistence farming. Lonely homesteads, a few small plots of barley and oats, thin channels cut in the peat to provide fresh water. These were difficult times for crofters, and a few had already sold out to Fountain. But what was alarming the Crofters Union more was a move towards speculative trading in crofting land. The holdings in this part of the Highlands were much bigger than those in the west, often several thousand acres in extent. Some had been purchased by outsiders, and there had been attempts to amalgamate and appropriate the common grazing so that this could be sold off for forestry. This was within the law of the 1976 Crofting Act, giving crofters the right to buy their holdings from the landlord for 15 times their annual rental, but quite against its spirit.

We drove to Andrew Cumming's holding by the Dubh Lochs of Shielton, along roads lined with narrow peat diggings, each with a handwritten sign giving the owner's name. Andrew gave us a cheerful elevenses, but was gloomy about afforestation, which he likened quite explicitly to the Clearances. 'They burned us then, now they are blanketing us' was his curt verdict.

Close to his homestead, now a feed store, men were fencing a new winter stock-pen. Nearby was a more ancient stockade, knitted together out of waste metal and old farm machinery – a frugal way of recycling rubbish that no one would ever bother to collect this far out. But beyond the farm on the bog itself, the marks of humans and nature were less easily distinguished. It was too late for most of the breeding waders. But the dark crossbow shapes of Arctic skuas skimmed across the swaying plumes of cotton grass, adding to that persistent impression that the entire land-scape was shifting.

Walking about in the oppressive humidity was a queasily disorientating experience. The sodden sphagnum rocked underfoot. It had an insubstantial, blubbery feel, like a jelly. Every square yard of it was different, a constantly re-shuffled mix of stag's horn lichens, sedges, and a dozen dif-ferent species of sphagnum, speckled with the sticky scarlet jaws of insectivorous sundews. The pools were different too, encrusted with moss, full of bogbean, or edged with the golden stars of bog asphodel. Thin sheets of rain swirl-ed in from the north-west blotting out first Sky Fea, and then the high Sutherland peaks to the west, until I hadn't the slightest idea in which direction I was facing. Several times that afternoon I had waves of inexplicable anxiety – something I'd often read American writers experiencing in wild places, but hadn't expected only 50 miles from In-verness. The bog was criss-crossed by cryptic trails and thin ribbons of seepage water, as if the sphagnum had cracked. They may have been natural, but the bog's skin is so fragile that it can show traces of damage for years. One was the track of an otter, a darting, decisive run that plunged into the pool, parted the bogbean and slithered out through the sedges on the far side.

But another that Lesley showed me was a human track-way, the old mail route that was until quite recently the postman's path across the bog. She told me a story that showed better than any abstract definition where the Flows lay on the scale between wilderness and wildness.

A few years ago a group of crofters were walking home along this trail in winter and became benighted. When they eventually reached a croft one of them was suffering badly from exposure. The others attempted to revive him by pressing hot stones against his feet, but overdid it, and suc-ceeded in burning his feet as well. In the end he had to be carried off the bog on a stretcher – out along the post road.

Time and again that day we saw what afforestation had done to 'this delicate economic and social fabric'. Croftlands had been flooded as a result of the diversion of water down drainage ditches. Silt from deep ploughing had been washed into salmon spawning areas. Pesticide and fertilizer run-off was polluting watercourses and streams.

Even the economics of the operation began to look shaky, especially when you have, in addition, to consider the damage from windthrow on this exposed plateau, and the ravages of the pine beauty moth, an endemic pest which chews alien pines (but not natives) to ribbons. Some of the trees were growing better than had been painted by conservationists, but only because of the forestry equivalent of intensive care. The National Audit Office, costing out the business the previous year, was scathing in its criticism. The real increase in the value of the trees was little more than one percent, which hardly justified the public subsidies being lavished upon them.

The *principle* that tree planting should be eligible for public money is obviously a commendable one. It means for instance that local authorities can establish and support native woodlands as amenities for their ratepayers. But from any political point of view it is a preposterous waste of public money as no public good accrues.

Scanning the list of names and figures on the land register I wondered what conservation benefit had been seen in Fountain's operation by Timothy Colman, an ex-member of the Countryside Commission and an NCC advisory committee in his 790 acres of afforested bog. Or whether Lady Porter, founder of the Westminster Against Reckless Spending campaign, felt there should be any cap on the £500,000 she was then legally entitled to in planting grants and tax relief.

Even the generation of jobs in the forestry sector looked like part of a prospector's dream. Fountain employed some 60 people in Caithness and Sutherland. The much-publicized figure of 2,000 jobs turned out to be a projection for 40 or 50 years hence, when the first trees would be due for felling and processing. Over the whole of the Highland region only 1,500 people were employed in the forestry and sawmilling industries, and a good deal of the work was done by outside contract labour, sometimes from as far afield as Germany.

Yet there were already models of a different kind of development here which respected the wildlife and crofting traditions of the peat plateau, but encouraged alternative agriculture and new small industries in the valleys. At Berriedale, north of Helmsdale, for example, there was a flourishing native woodland of birch, oak and rowan, a spring water bottling plant, and an experimental wind generator (the local authorities wanted this to be painted conifer green, but it remained a defiant airy cream above the open moors).

*

I travelled home from Sutherland the long way, hoping to write a first draft of my article *en route*. Out of the train window I kept catching glimpses of the North Sea, itself under siege from over-fishing and pollution, and a reminder that the exploitation of wild places is no local problem. Between pages I dipped into Barry Lopez's wonderful celebration of northern landscapes, *Arctic Dreams*, to try and get a wider perspective on the Flows issue. 'Confronted by an unknown landscape,' he had written, 'what happens to our sense of wealth? What does it mean to grow rich?' I hoped we were becoming wise enough as a people not to regard land as waste or sterile just because it had no overriding economic use. The Flow Country was already rich beyond accounting. Perhaps only a lucky few would see its wading birds, as they flew down to Africa. But its sub-arctic wastes, teeming with birds on the long summer evenings, was one of the great landscapes of the imagination, an engine of life for the whole northern hemisphere.

If the foresters were sceptical about this it would do them no harm to wait a decade or two till the arguments had settled. The peatlands had no such choice. They were the product of thousands of years of evolution and could never be recreated in our time.

The Backwoods

1

Hardings Wood lies just above the western end of the ridgeway, a raggedy, up-and-down patch surrounded by pasture
and old hedges. I bought it in 1981, and was too excited at
the time to realize that the landscapes along the track still
had a spell over me. There was, I suppose, some poetic justice in this. Having grown up at one end, cursing farmers
and muttering charms amongst the trees, I had ended up at
the other, a landholder with deeds and neighbours' fences
to think about.

I have been commuting along this western stretch a
couple of times a week since then and the trip has come to
feel like a carriage drive, back to the ancestral seat. But it
never stops seeming like a rite of passage too. The last mile
of the trackway meanders along below the extreme edge of
the Chilterns, with the steep chalk escarpment on the one
hand and the Vale of Aylesbury on the other, and travelling
regularly across this frontierland has given me a new view
of my home countryside. Even in the three miles between
town and wood there is a sense of geology and history rolling back. Just past the last executive villas and a belt of tidy
arable enclosures, the road narrows and begins to tilt down.
You drop into a twisting tunnel of hazel and hornbeam,
edged with drifts of flint where cars have repeatedly gouged
into the banks. Tiers of wooded embankments, covered
with anemones and woodruff, drop away towards the Vale;
and in spring the tunnel fills with a soft green light filtering
in from the west.

Through gaps in the hedges you can catch glimpses of
the next peninsula of ragged woodland jutting out into the
Vale. On its crest are the gorse and birch sweeps of Berkhamsted Common, and odd-shaped fields hacked out of its
edges in medieval times. From this distance they look no
more than doodlings on a vast and bristling green pelt. It's a
view which often makes me smile at the belief that the landscape is a purely man-made artefact.

Then, when the lane has burrowed almost to the valley

bottom it splits in two and corkscrews round through nearly 150 degrees to begin climbing back – due south, into the hill country. From here I can see my patch, Hardings Wood, squatting close to the top of the hill, a green tump with abrupt edges that looks as if it was once destined for bigger things. Round this corner you are into a different country – and a different climate. I have driven into blizzards and black ice here when it seemed like a mild winter's day only a hundred yards away in the valley. Even in high summer when the hill pastures are beginning to crack, there is a soft, humid feel in the ferny gulleys. Welcome to the Chilterns.

The ridgeway has always marked a kind of boundary between the tamed valley lands and wilder woods to the south. It is probably neolithic in origins, and even the dense hedges that line it are more than a thousand years old. This western section was called Shokersweye in the fourteenth century, which was sweetened to Sugarsway in the late eighteenth century, and Shootersway in Victorian times. Local mythology has its origins as a strangers' or robbers' track, a dangerous alternative to the main road in the valley. But the legend of an infamous past is probably just part of the old argument about what constitutes rural security – the Celtic fondness for high ground and woody enclaves versus the Roman belief in valley towns, good roads and discipline.

The Roman view, that 'the forest' is incompatible with civilization, still has the edge, and colours our views of both present and past. Before the last war, when the extent of human impact on our landscape wasn't fully realized, the Ordnance Survey speckled their reconstructed maps of Anglo-Saxon Britain with tracts of impenetrable oak forest. In the more technologically minded sixties and seventies, when the countryside began to be looked on as a man-made garden and estimations of the population of Dark Age Britain soared, the mapped forest beat a dramatic retreat. Only now are we beginning to come to terms with the notion that our ancestors were able to lead cultured lives *in-*

side woods; and that civilization, far from being the converse of wilderness, may actually need it to survive.

The argument has always seemed a distant one to me. I grew up amongst woods and have always taken them for granted as natural sites for most of life's pleasures. When I began to rediscover my Chiltern roots in the seventies – this time with an appreciation that they had a past as well as a present – it was largely by way of an intensive period of wood-crawling.

Once again the weather had a hand in things. In retrospect the curious, unseasonable winters of the mid-seventies may have been a first taste of the unpredictable weather that was to follow in the eighties. They were mild, damp and oppressive, 1974 especially. In the autumn of that year a pall of cloud and misling rain arrived in late September and stayed till March. I had taken the plunge of becoming a full-time writer just a year before, and was feeling more weather-vulnerable than usual. I sat gazing at unfilled pages in the typewriter, blaming the gloom outside for fogging my brain – and then cursing my mood for making the days outside seem even more claustrophobic. Normally, I could be shamed out of these sulky vicious circles by an early celandine, or just by catching the single-minded eye of a blackbird defying the gloom. But that winter the natural world seemed to be suffering a block of its own. Toadstools hung about in the woods, turning into white balls of mildew, fungi infested by fungi. A film of green algae grew so thickly over tree trunks that it became hard to tell one species from another. And, in a limp parody of spring, grasses sprung from seedheads still anchored at the top of last-year's stalks, and sprawled like creepers over the hedges.

I remember seeing Ian Nairn, on one of his maverick journeys about Europe for BBC television, saunter into the Black Forest, throw his arms round a tree and murmur, 'I could have done with a wood like this a few times before'. Woods are the best antidote to winter depression. Being naturally dark places from early summer to autumn, much of their inner life goes on in late winter, when the branches are still bare and the light is strongest. Tits and finches flock at this time, feeding on nuts and torpid grubs. The first bluebell shoots are often showing by mid-January and the first woodland blossom of the year, the waxy-yellow spurge laurel, in full flower by the end of the month.

That winter I felt I needed a more drastic treatment than a stroll round the local copses, so I began exploring the Chiltern woods further south during long lunchtime truancies from my desk. I would drive down to isolated pubs in the country between Watlington and Hambledon, sit in the bar and scribble – or more often make plans for scribbling. In the hour or so of what passed for daylight after lunch I'd meander off, down lanes and woodland tracks that, after the long rains, all seemed to be some variation on the theme of a twisted rut between bare beech roots. Yet there was an intriguing quirkiness about the region, a sense that it hadn't been got the measure of, that you might just stand a chance of getting lost. That motif – a clawed root hugging a steep bank, and a track or strip of pasture below, also clinging precariously on to a slope – was the signature of the place.

When the spring came and the gloom began to lift I would drive up to the wooded commons between Naphill and Hampden or the steeps round Turville, just for a break in the afternoon's work. By the time the great heatwave of 1975 had arrived I was more familiar with beechwoods than I had ever been as a child. I was working on a book with the photographer Tony Evans at the time, a cultural history of our flora called *The Flowering of Britain*, and we spent many days that summer scouring the woods for orchids.

A beechwood in high summer is a wood reduced to its bare essentials – ground, trunk and leaves. The shade is so all-encompassing that there are few young trees, no shrubs, and, except for the early spring, only a scattering of ground plants. The canopy muffles sound, too, so that often the only thing you hear is the soft scuffing of your own footsteps in last year's leaves. This is the kind of situation to which woodland orchids are best adapted. Many of them are partial parasites, and make little their own chlorophyll. They haunt dark corners, feeding on decaying vegetation and animal remains, living strange, fugitive existences that are more like fungi than flowers. Most are southerly species that revel in the heat.

That baking summer of 1975 the ghost orchid – so slow-growing and finnicky in its requirements that it may flower only once every 20 years – bloomed pallidly in a remote Chiltern wood. And a clump of soldier orchids (so called because their flowers bear a slight resemblance to a man in tunic and helmet) was found in wood close by, after supposedly being extinct in Britain for 30 years. It was a sensational rediscovery, and when the local conservation trust put the plant under a high security, round-the-clock guard, even the popular press became fascinated. For the *Daily Mirror*'s reporter it meant 'a pledge of secrecy, a rendezvous in a car park off a lonely country road . . . a long walk, a last few careful steps' and there, as the grainy black-and-white photograph was captioned, 'The Beauty that must Blossom in Secret'.

I gradually learned the knack of tracking down the commoner woodland species. They were a cryptic, retiring collection. The flowers of the fly orchid are like small, velvet-bodied beetles impaled on the stem. The bird's-nest orchid's are the colour of honeycombs and old beech leaves. The helleborines are so slender and muted in colour that you have to search for them close to the ground, looking for the vertical lines that break the vacuum of shade beneath the beeches. All of them needed almost to be stalked, and they seemed to me to be perfect companion plants for these secretive, surprising woods.

These days I settle for shorter walks. One especially seems to capture the essence of the Chilterns. It is a circular tramp down in the valley of the Chess, only ten miles from Berkhamsted and 15 from London. Yet compared to walks on the home patch it has a luxuriant, southerly feel. The swallows arrive sooner and the bluebells bloom earlier. On warm days in late April, a south-east breeze blows the smell of balsam poplar buds right up the valley. It is a place I often escape to when a ritual plod round the Top seems too clogged with stale memories or northern reserve. One May, I saw the actual beginning of spring here, and felt for a moment like a witch-doctor whose spell had worked. There had been nearly 24 hours of cool, heavy rain and I had driven down to the Chess to try and get beyond it. I sat on a log by the side of the river and watched the cloud begin to lift. Small bands of swifts and martins appeared, drifting in high from the south. Then – it seemed to happen in the space of a few seconds – the wind veered round to the south-east. It was like an oxygen-mask being clamped to the face, so sudden and inspiriting that I looked at my watch for the time. It went down in my diary: '6th May, 1978. Spring quickening, 4 p.m. exactly'.

The walk itself is ordinary enough – through a string of meadows on one side of the river and back along the foot of a steep beechwood on the other. But the river here snakes through a complicated series of S-bends and creeks, and has squeezed its surroundings – water meadows, tangled marshes, scraps of wood – into an incongruous jumble. Everything seems on the point of changing into something else. Hedgerows that date back to before the Norman Conquest crowd into meadows full of oil-barrel pony jumps. Watercress beds edge into the woods, and waterside flowers sometimes nip up the bank to colonize the gaps formed when tall beech and hornbeams come down in gales. The woodland retaliates, and the glutinous white caps of porcelain fungus sprout like waterlilies from wind-thrown beech branches in the stream. Trees fall so frequently here that the path through the hanging wood has become a kind of scenic steeplechase, with new views every year. One June it was a flock of sheep up to their ears in yellow flags; in the autumn of 1989 an extraordinary corner decked out in red: a summer-house at the edge of a field, surrounded by late-season cherry leaves, and with a scarlet stock-car parked in front of it. Late one April evening I saw six cuckoos together in one of the meadows, swooping down into the grass from their perches on the previous year's willowherb. Ganging up like this is the way that normally solitary cuckoos celebrate a good caterpillar find after migration. Dashing about amid the running water and the high hedges they looked as if they had alighted on a treasure island.

This festive air infects the people who come here, too. It is a popular walk, over land with untypically tolerant owners, and is strewn with people when the weather is fine. Some are picnicking, but it is the kind of place where sleeping and Socratic debate and sheer eccentricity don't seem in the least out of order. One regular plods the circuit in climbing boots, carrying a small dog in his arms. Another comes to photograph wild flowers, and kneels in front of them as if in astonishment that they should open in his presence. Two others I have never seen, but their champagne glasses sit, perfectly polished, high up in the cruck of a huge pollard oak. I once crossed paths with a party of sixth-formers from a Jewish school in north London by this tree. It was their first visit, and they wanted to make sure of getting back to Chorleywood station without missing any of the scenery. Could I point them along a quick but interesting route? I did my best and we went our separate ways. Half an hour later I spotted them again, well on schedule, marching in single file in the high wood with their Hebrew songs ringing through the beeches.

Does the *genius loci* help shape the behaviour and character of the people who live with it? It certainly seems to attract kindred spirits. The dense, muddled landscapes of the Chilterns have a long history as a refuge for nonconformist religious and political movements. Amersham was a stronghold of the Lollards in the sixteenth century. The Levellers had groups here during the English Revolution (and gave that thrilling title – *A Light Shining in Buckinghamshire* – to their most celebrated pamphlet). The Chartists created a settlement of 35 smallholdings at Heronsgate, near Chorleywood, and Jordans, near Beaconsfield, began in 1919 as a Quaker-inspired village for craftsmen and women.

The tradition has taken some unexpected turns recently. At the end of the seventies a Buddhist monastery was set up on a farm on the edge of the Ashridge estate. The monks are a familiar sight with their shaved pates and pale robes, billowing about Berkhamsted Common or going on shopping expeditions in their minibus. Early in 1986 I was contacted by one of the senior monks, who was anxious to discuss how they should look after a patch of woodland they had acquired with the farm. It sounded a rather worldly business, and I was pleased to do some walking and get acquainted before we had to tackle it.

It was the second coldest February this century. Daytime temperatures barely rose above freezing for the whole month, and we crunched our way towards the wood over inches of frozen snow. My host was an American who had spent some time in the Far East and, despite the cold, he seemed wrapped in a protecting aura of aromatic herbs. Here and there the snow was pitted with orange stains, rather unsettlingly close to the colour of his robes. I wondered for a moment if they were watery bloodstains, the last traces of ravenous encounters in the dead of night, but soon realized that they had come from the droppings of roosting fieldfares and redwings that had been surviving on a diet of hips and haws.

Not entirely on berries, my host corrected me. He told me that the community had been feeding the birds during the freeze-up – though only with strictly macrobiotic titbits. The local birds had taken a while to get accustomed, but now snapped up brown rice like devout initiates. In Thailand, where he had been a novice, the birds had found bread quite incomprehensible.

We reached the part of the wood he was concerned about. It was a typical Chiltern patch, some old cherries and hornbeams, stands of 150-year-old beech in natural, forky shapes, and a few gaps with regenerating ash and sycamore. My host said that what they really wanted were some glades, and was this possible without harming the wood? I thought it was, though it would normally be done by taking out what foresters called the 'mature' (meaning early middle-aged) trees, and that I wondered if he was thinking of anything so extreme. He confessed he wasn't, and at last explained what the purpose of the whole exercise was. The community needed somewhere for the novices to practise their chanting, out of earshot of each other and of the traffic in the surrounding lanes, and he thought that the shelter of a woodland glade would be ideal. We wandered on and found plenty of patches of youngish sycamore and ash that could be cut out to make room for a few cells. I left, savouring the prospect of mantras amongst the bluebells and hermits back in the woods for the first time since they were fashionable accessories on the estates of the eighteenth-century poseurs.

All kinds of refugees have found their niche amongst the combes and added to their sense of being a frontierland. I have met an escaped emu galloping up a lane, a lonely accordionist playing Irish lilts on the edge of a common, and an eccentric White Russian fungus collector with a highly original interpretation of the Revolution. Champneys Health Farm, next to my wood, regularly disgorges bands of gaudily track-suited and cosmopolitan joggers into the nearby lanes. But these are dullards by the side of the distinguished African chief who stayed at the Farm a few years ago. He was very tall and very wide, and, dressed in a pure white ankle-length robe, would shuffle slowly along the lanes. He was accompanied by a line of what I assume were wives, identically dressed and following about ten paces behind. This stately procession was visible half a mile away and moved so elegantly that at times they appeared to be gliding above the winter hedges.

But it is the Celtic echoes that are the loudest, and not just because the Celts were amongst the earliest settlers. The landscape itself has a western feel, and is full of curves and romantic flourishes. The writer H.J. Massingham, who loved Celtic cultures second only to Classical and longed to find relics of them in his beloved Chilterns, became convinced that a celebrated chalk hill carving at Watlington, not far from the Icknield Way, was an authentic Celtic fertility symbol. In 1940 he wrote: 'The White Mark is a pyramid about 86 feet high and the base 16 feet across, the apex pointing SSE so that the sun, rising over the hill, possibly at the midsummer equinox, would strike it. This apex of the pyramid, which is remarkably like the ghostly shadow of a church spire lying along the hill, ends in a diamond, and it may well be that here is an original pointer to that most potent of the heavenly bodies, from some 2000 to 2500 years older than Shakespeare's "shepherds dials".'

Massingham's ghostly simile was closer to the truth than he realized. The Watlington White Mark was cut by an eighteenth-century landscaper. Mr Horne could see Watlington church from his window, and felt it would be improved by a spire. So he had the image of one carved in the chalk in Watlington Hill, in such a way that, from his window, church and fake spire lined up as one.

The origins of the most famous Chiltern hill carving, the Whipsnade Lion, are just as mundane. It was carved on the Downs at Dunstable in 1935 as an advertisement for nearby Whipsnade Zoo. Yet it is an awesome, prowling beast, covering over an acre and a half of chalk, and glares out so conspicuously over the Vale that it had to be covered with bracken during the war. Now its outline is lit up with 750 sponsored 40 watt light bulbs. There have always been jokes in fields here, with the apparently immemorial sometimes turning out, on closer inspection, to be just a memorial.

I think we sometimes read too much reverence and order into ancient artefacts, and forget that they were often made for humdrum domestic reasons, and occasionally just for fun. People have always chipped away at the chalk, to leave their mark, needle the gentry, get one back at nature. And the landscape – rather like language in that it is hard to tell when we are its creatures and when its creators – chips away at us. Adam Nicholson caught the two-way nature of this relationship when he called such anciently engraved land-scapes 'psychosomatic'.

2

The basic character of the Chilterns is a fact of geology and ecology that humans haven't yet been able to obscure. Drive towards them from the west, along the M40, and when you are still five miles away they stretch from one end of the horizon to the other, a dark, indomitable ridge of tree-clad chalk, like a first glimpse of the Lost Plateau.

The region was 'Cilterne' (hill country) to the Celts; and the two words may come from a common root meaning hill or high. Even in Saxon times it was wild country, and the twentieth-century expression 'Taking the Chiltern Hun-dreds', used of a member of Parliament when he wishes to resign his seat, is a hangover from this time when the region was so remote and lawless that special Crown Stewards were appointed to oversee it.

Yet compared to, say, the Cotswolds or the South Downs, it is an unknown country, and you can drive straight across its 400 square miles on one of the major through-roads and barely realize you've been there. Guide-books are apt to explain this by likening the region to a clenched fist, pointing west. The few gaps through which the scarce rivers and major roads run are represented by the lines between the fingers and knuckles. Between them is a network of deep gulleys and combes that is almost invisible from the main roads. They are mostly waterless, heavily wooded and hard to cultivate.

There is chalk, of course, underlying the whole range, and it has produced stretches of downland turf along the scarp, especially round Ivinghoe and Dunstable. But the quintessential substances of the Chilterns are clay and flint. I think we glimpsed this as children, when gathering flints and walking over them was an essential part of getting to grips with the landscape. They seem inexhaustible in the fields, and after heavy rains the smaller pieces wash out into the lanes and pile up like miniature shingle beaches. In the drier woods, huge pieces sometimes seem to appear over-night on the top of steep slopes, as if they had mysteriously bobbed up through the clay.

No one knows exactly how flint is formed, except that it begins with the same shells and skeletons of sea creatures that formed the chalk itself. Somehow the siliceous matter is dissolved out and redeposited as this hard, lustrous, almost glass-like rock, one of the most complete transmuta-tions of living matter it is possible to imagine. But the chalk can have the last word. I once found a thin cylinder of flint in the rough shape of a spearhead. There was a small circle scalloped out of the side, and a hole in its centre into which the soft chalk had seeped and formed a perfect white heart, set in the steel-grey stone.

If flint is the commonplace Chiltern rock, puddingstone is the talisman. It is a very local rock, a conglomerate of all kinds of pebbles and dross, packed together by the glaciers like a natural concrete. Vast lumps of this are sometimes turned up by the plough, especially from ground being broken for the first time. It adorns village greens and pub counters, but is reckoned to be lucky (bits were once sold as 'toadstone') and most of these public rocks are gradually shrinking. Some even do mysterious post-glacial (and usually nocturnal) migrations into back gardens.

*

It is the beechwoods that define the Chilterns in most people's eyes. Plantations of pure beech cover a third of the land surface in the south-west of the region. More ex-pansive free-standing trees line field boundaries and arch over tracks. On wooded commons on the clay plateaux there are immense beech pollards, shaped by centuries of lopping. They are all loved (coddled, sometimes) and seen as essential to the Chiltern's identity. They are also wrapped up in dense layers of mythology and what Oliver Rackham calls 'pseudo-history'.

The uniform stands of smooth-barked, straight-trunked, high-branching trees – 'natural cathedrals' is the hushed guidebook description – are, for a start, neither natural nor immemorial. A thousand years ago the tree cover of the Chilterns included a fair amount of rough beech, but was a vastly more diverse woodland, with oak, ash, maple and elm as well. Most of it was worked as coppice. The move towards selecting out beech for growing as timber, and then finally towards planting beech, only began in the early nineteenth century, to serve the burgeoning Windsor chair industry in High Wycombe.

But now, if the warnings of foresters are to be believed, these plantations – and, by implication, the whole fabric of the Chiltern landscape – are in a state of crisis. Weakened by drought, chomped by grey squirrels, strangled by scrub, the beech mantle is about to fall apart. The Chilterns Standing Conference has described the local beeches as 'ageing and degenerating' (as if such processes were unnatural, or not quite decent) and advised that massive replanting is the only answer. One local woodland management group recruits supporters and funds with the slogan: 'The Chiltern trees are dying! The work must go on or the Chiltern woodland will rot away', a prophesy that makes one wonder how on earth trees were ever able to cover Britain before the invention of foresters.

What is happening out in the beechwoods is rather less apocalyptic. There is erosion from disease, squirrels, and weather, but it is rarely fatal. It reduces the commercial value of the timber, but in many ways the growers have only themselves to blame, for tree monocultures are just as vulnerable to these kinds of afflictions as arable prairies. When trees do succumb they are immediately surrounded by hosts of ambitious seedlings, sometimes beech, but if not, always ash and birch. If left these will gradually grow into a more natural – and more resilient – mixed tree cover. But they are repeatedly sprayed or cut out as 'scrub'. It is not the woodland cover of the Chilterns that is in danger, so much as our self-regarding, static image of what it should be like.

Behind the dramatic warnings is an assumption that is obstinately deep-rooted in our culture: that trees are not natural, self-sufficient growths, but human artefacts, woody pets, that rely on planting and pampering for their very existence. It is an assumption that says more about our attitudes towards nature than about the life of trees.

*

The Chiltern beechwood that I have come to know best could never be mistaken for a planted conceit. Frithsden Beeches on Berkhamsted Common is one of the most remarkable examples of a beech wood-pasture in the country. It is a catacomb of immense, contorted pollards, natural gargoyles and grotesques, chilling tricks of the light, and, increasingly these days, a riot of wrecked trunks and branches – gale-strewn, frost-cracked, split sometimes from end to end. It isn't much like a natural cathedral but it is defiantly alive; and its long history casts some light on the origins of our paternalistic attitudes towards trees, and on what we may be losing by trying to keep them under such a close rein.

There has probably been a wood here since the last Ice Age, and it may have been a wood of beech pollards for half that time. Pollarding is a technique for reconciling the harvesting of wood (chiefly for fuel in the case of beech) with the grazing of cattle, and was introduced to this country by Mediterranean settlers 4,000 or 5,000 years ago. The top growth of the tree was cut back on a regular rotation at about eight to ten feet up – above the height at which animals could browse away the new branches sprouting around the cuts. This meant that stock could safely be allowed to graze under the trees and take advantage of the flush of grass produced by the increased light. In later years, as the new branches grew more mature, there would be mast (beech nuts) as well.

The trees that developed under this regime were short-trunked, broad-backed, set on immense root braces, and decorated with intricate flutings, knobs and scars where the bark had grown back over the cut surfaces. But in their younger years at least, the trunks still had some timber value. In 1353, in a doubly impudent action, the Black Prince took and sold a large number of the beeches from 'the foreign woods' of Frithsden so that he could buy oak timber for fencing off another part of the common as a private deer park.

The early 1600s (about the time the oldest of Frithsden's surviving individual trees were growing from seed) saw more attempts at enclosing the common. Most were illegal and were thwarted by the commoners, who destroyed the fences. But in the late eighteenth and early nineteenth centuries, the pressure to tidy up and discipline the common grew more intense. Various well-known landscapers, including Capability Brown and Humphry Repton, were called in to work around the estate, but thankfully did little more than cut open some straight rides and long distance views of the rather vulgar manor house at Ashridge. It was the economical edge of the philosophy of Improvement that was a bigger threat to the character and communal role of the Beeches.

In the eighteenth century tree planting had become a passion among the landed classes. It was seen as a patriotic duty and a way of 'dignifying the look of the land'. It combined estate beautification with sound investment, and made a powerful symbolic statement about the planter's social status and its likely inheritance down through the generations – for at least as long as the life of a hardwood tree. Repton himself reckoned that nothing excelled it for those who wanted to display their territorial power and what he called their 'appropriation' of the landscape. But if these ambitions were to succeed it was important that no one else 'appropriated' or disfigured any of the estate's trees, and rights of pollarding were outlawed in many places at this time. This didn't happen at Frithsden but plantations began to appear round the fringes of the common, including stands of beeches that were very different from the squat, vernacular, workhorse pollards. These new beeches were like Palladian columns in wood, tasteful, aristocratic beeches, beeches as capital.

In 1865 the young Lord Brownlow (to whom the whole Ashridge estate had passed) drew up a scheme for the 'improvement' of the common under the General Enclosure Act. His plan was to enclose some 400 acres of the common, including Frithsden Beeches, and clear them for cultivation and timber plantations. His agents were able to get more than 400 signatures in support of the plan from local inhabitants with the promise of a 40-acre recreation ground alongside the canal in Berkhamsted. But he failed to get the approval of all the commoners, including the crucially influential Augustus Smith, 'Lord of the Scilly Isles', who was well-known for championing public rights to the foreshore in the Scillies. When Brownlow decided not to wait for the legal niceties to be completed and put four miles of fencing round the common, Smith retaliated in kind. He hired a band of 130 London navvies, who came up by train on the night of March 6th, marched up to the common and pulled the railings down. The next day, as reported in the press, 'the news spread, and the inhabitants of the adjacent village and district flocked to the scene. In carriages, gigs, dogcarts, and on foot, gentry, shopkeepers, husbandmen, women and children, at once tested the reality of what they saw by strolling over and squatting on the Common and taking away morsels of gorse to prove, as they said, the place was their own again.'

It was an extraordinary event, the full story of which is told in Lord Eversley's book *Commons, Forests and Footpaths* (1910). Lord Brownlow swiftly took out an action for damages against Smith, but died before the case came to court. Meanwhile, Smith mounted a counter suit for illegal enclosure, which eventually triumphed after more than three years of litigation. The outcome (which marked an historic precedent for the burgeoning commons preservation movement) was that most of the extant rights of grazing, cutting fern and gorse, etc., on the common were given legal standing. The one which was not registered, ironically, was the right to cut firewood from the pollards. The practice had died out just a few years before, when the newly opened railway and canal began bringing coal to the neighbourhood at one third of the price of firewood.

The pollards have not been cut since, and have grown into a collection of highly distinctive characters. A few have names and all are instantly recognizable as individuals. One has what can only be described as an immense paunch, a corpulent layer of woody tissue formed to contain a canker. Another has a maze of fused and ingrowing branches that looks exactly like a cut-away diagram of an intestine. It helps that they are all naturally sprung and have a very broad genetic ancestry. There are naturally lumpy trunks, fluted trunks, smooth and fissured barks, Classical, Gothic and Perpendicular branchings, even one or two copper-leaved sports. And as they grow, everything that has happened to them – lopping and deer nibbling; attacks by gales, lightning, woodpeckers; sapwood-fattening springs and summer droughts; swaddling by moss and the steady seeping of fungal juices into their heartwood – has been incorporated, ingrained, in their structure. So have their staunch efforts (successful, usually) to heal over breaches in their defences. Trees do not age or 'degenerate' in the same way as humans. What we, anthropomorphically, describe as 'damage' may be nothing of the kind. A large branch torn off a trunk may be a chink by which fungal spores can enter; but it can just as likely reduce the tree's top-heaviness and actually prolong its life, as pollarding does. Where bark grows back over a wound in the sapwood, it doesn't become angular or senescent, but rounded, generous, conciliatory. On many of the beeches at Frithsden it is possible to see the bosses where the very last branches were lopped, a century and a half ago. They are surprisingly small, as smooth as turned wood – historical time capsules, but also part of the irrepressible living surface of the wood.

Ironically, the ending of pollarding spelt the eventual

downfall of the beeches. Whilst they were still cut every 20 years or so, their leaf canopies were kept relatively small and compact. After a century and half they have formed an immense superstructure, awesome to look at, but too top-heavy for the short and ageing trunks. Increasing numbers come down every time there is a high wind, along with their extraordinary cargoes: old nests, mattresses of leaf-mould accumulated in deep forks, and sometimes small trees which had rooted in this and been growing 30 feet above the ground. I once went round the Beeches with a party of woodland owners and foresters who were outraged that such an array of 'freaks', as they called them, had been given living room for so long. 'They are rubbish,' growled a local major, 'an insult to the forester's craft'. Fortunately, the National Trust (the present owner) understands the unique character of the pollards and the affection that is felt for them locally. It has ignored puritanical pleas for their clearance and has appeased the more practical anxieties of its insurance company with a ring of notices warning the public of the dangers of wind-blown branches.

But, dangers notwithstanding, the start of the gale season is the best time to be there. In December the leaves are gone, the ground water has started to rise, and that muffling heaviness of a beechwood in high summer has been blown away. Almost everything is on the move. I try, not always successfully, to keep my eyes on the swaying branches as well as the debris on the ground, and often walk halfway past the deer that are standing, stock still, amongst the thickets of young saplings, every face pointed tensely towards me. We stare each other out for a few minutes. Then the cord breaks and they stream out towards the open common, a ribbon of chamois, mottled fawn and leaf-mould brown that seems to have picked up all the colours of a winter beechwood.

Meanwhile, the next generation of trees is creeping remorselessly back the other way. In the borderlands between the Beeches and the bracken, and wherever a pollard has fallen, there are stands of silver birch grown from windblown seed, mixed with bird-sown beech, cherry, holly and oak. The young beech grows in shelves, like a roughly clipped and layered hedge, reflecting the fact that beech mast is only plentiful once every four or five years, and that the deer browse away any new growth within reach. They will always keep the rides and glades open because of this, but the young trees are winning and when the last pollard falls, they will make up the natural tree cover of the Beeches.

I always visit a favourite tree that came down in a gale early in 1986. We knew it as the Praying Beech, from two branches which had fused in the form of a pair of hands clasped across the trunk. It came down in dramatic style, half yanked clear out of the ground, half split across its four-foot-diameter trunk just above the ground. Inside it was already half rotten, and from the charred wood close to the heart, looked as if it had grown right round an ancient fire or lightning strike. It was sad when it fell, but it has barely lost any of its character, propped up as it is with its root in the air. Bees have nested in the stump, and wrens amongst the tangle of vegetation round the root plate. The entreating hands (they will last for a few decades yet), now point directly down at the ground, and have successfully summoned up hosts of fungi to begin the slow task of turning the tree back into earth. They seem almost to be embroidering the trunk, knots of purple *Coryne* and yellow *Bisporella*, tufts of dead men's fingers and stag's horn, waxy brocades of coral spot pricked through the bark.

Like most of the other pollards it is also decorated with carved graffiti. They are not to everyone's taste, but carving initials in the soft bark of beech trees is an ancient custom that even has a classical proverb to its credit: '*Crescent illae; crescetis amores*' – as these letters grow so may our love. At Frithsden there are the initials of US Airmen stationed in the area during the Second World War, the linked pledges of sweethearts from the outbreak of the First, and elegant signatures from the Victorian period, now so stretched that it is impossible to be sure of any before 'RG

1876'. The trees are no more perturbed by these inscriptions than by any of the other problems of cohabitation that face them every day. They are all simply absorbed.

The question that is asked more urgently with every storm is whether pollarding itself should be resumed to try and prolong the life of the remaining trees. Alas, after a century and a half without cutting it is doubtful if they could stand the shock of abrupt decapitation. One alternative way of providing continuity might be to pollard some of the younger, self-sown beeches, and the National Trust has already begun some tentative experiments with squirrel-damaged trees. But the large-scale lopping of healthy young trees (commonplace when there was still an economic need for the wood) would be a more contentious business. In a climate of opinion that regards trees as being killed if they are cut and incapable of growing unless they are planted, the idea that we could live with them rather as honeysuckle does – up close, in harness, breaking or bending the odd branch to our own advantage but basically just using them as a free-standing, independent framework for part of our life – is still looked on as something close to betrayal.

3

No doubt all kinds of sublimated longings lurked behind the desire that welled up in me in the late seventies to have a wood of my own. I was not far off middle age, had lost my bolt-hole in East Anglia, and was finding the whole business of freelance writing increasingly lonely and precarious. A bosky retreat rather more ancient than myself would have been anyone's sensible prescription. But on the surface the ambition seemed more mundanely practical. I simply wanted somewhere where I could put all this woodland theorizing to the test. I could see the scene quite clearly: the parish out coppicing in the winter sun, the wood responding with floods of spring flowers and seedling trees, the 'Private' notices consigned to the bonfire (except those against the local hunt and the conifer barons), the Greenwood restored to the People. The one blemish in this utopian fantasy was that to disown a wood, so to speak, I would first have to own one, and play the property game.

I began looking around, but most of the local woods that were small enough to be in my price range were either part of big estates or already owned by forestry companies and shooting syndicates. In the end there seemed to be just one possible site within the four-mile radius from home I had set as my limit. It was called Hardings Wood, and was a dark and seemingly abandoned 16-acre patch close to the house of my friends Francesca and John in the next village of Wigginton. I knew it slightly and it seemed perfect, obviously ancient and potentially full of wildlife, but dark and forbidding enough to provide ample opportunities for heroic rescue work. And, with Fran and John close by, there would always be someone to keep an eye on it.

By the spring of 1981 I had made the decision to try to track down the owner and see if he or she wanted to dispose of it. Then a 'For Sale' notice appeared pinned to a tree by the entrance. Hardings was going on the market as the smallest lot in a large parcel of local woods. This was the first of a series of coincidences that eased the strain of the nail-biting weeks that followed. I put in a bid for what I imagined the wood was worth only to be told it was derisory. The agents quickly realized that they were dealing with a potential purchaser motivated by irrational emotions and not hard commercial sense, and never budged from their asking price. They were quite right. It was spring time, the wood was awash with bluebells, and having made a commitment I found I was already besotted by the place. I raised my bid and waited. Throughout that spring I sat under the trees, dreaming of what I would do with the place, and plunging into misery every time I spotted another visitor with clipboard and Norfolk jacket. I eventually discovered (by another extraordinary stroke of luck: a piece of wayward photocopying on the back of a quite unconnected piece of correspondence) that someone else was bidding for the whole parcel of woods, and that his forestry adviser was a man I knew slightly. By now I was convinced that fate intended me to have the wood. I threw protocol aside and wrote the adviser a begging letter saying that Hardings was surely too small and rough to be of any interest to a commercial forester, and that if they left it out of their block purchase I could guarantee it a good home. They did, and in August 1981, it became officially my property.

What one did next I wasn't entirely sure, but the wood itself seemed full of prompts. It was not so much one wood as three. Straddling a steepish valley that felt as if it ought to carry a stream (it probably had once, when the Chilterns were being formed), was a mixture chiefly of tall ash, cherry, and hazel. The slope flattened into a dry and flinty plateau with hornbeam, beech, sessile oak and holly growing free-range, as they might on a common. And to the north, separated from this old part of the wood by a wide bank and ditch, was a plantation of 90-year-old beeches. There was a pond with frogs, a labyrinthine badger sett and a spectacular range of ancient woodland plants: yellow archangel, wood anemone, spurge laurel, three varieties of woodland orchid, and ferns that were almost unknown elsewhere in Hertfordshire.

But the overriding feeling of the wood was one of emptiness and dark. There were no paths and no shrubs to speak of. There were not even any seedling trees, and though the flowers were rich, they were patchy. What had gone wrong? As far as I could tell Hardings, like many small woods, had been pretty well gutted of timber during the last war, and the closely packed trees that grew there now had regenerated naturally from the cut stumps or from seed. At some time during the fifties the previous owner had interplanted these with stands of hybrid Italian poplars. It was a bizarre choice, given that these non-native trees only really prosper on damp, rich soils. But in those days Bryant and May were sponsoring the growing of poplars for matchwood, and could have encouraged some speculative planting. Then the wood was virtually abandoned. There was no thinning of the closely packed mixture of wild and planted trees, and they grew leggy and tall. The poplars fared especially badly. They became infested with honey fungus, whose long rhizomes creep like black leather thongs under the bark and eventually kill them, and on the dry steep slopes they had already started to topple over. In many places they had formed mattresses of spongy rotting wood which was blotting out all life beneath.

What the wood needed above all was to be set free from this legacy of mismanagement, to be allowed to develop its natural structure, to have some light let in. It also needed some more human company. When I first took round a party of children from the local primary school, I was astonished to find that none of them had ever been in the wood before, even though it was less that a third of a mile from the village. But the children gave me an invaluable lesson in not making too many assumptions about what the wood should be like and what people might want from it. I had taken them to see the entrances to the vast badger sett, which range along a hundred yards of creeper-draped chalk bank at the edge of the wood. But they were more interested in the clump of naturalized laurel at the top of the bank, where they had found the long scratch marks that badgers make when they are sharpening their claws. Garden laurel would normally be one of the first intruders you would clear out of an ancient wood, but, watching the children snaking about amongst the twisted trunks searching for scratches, I realized that both they and the badgers had staked out a solid claim for their retention.

Early that autumn I began canvassing the village. I was able to place a few articles about the wood and my plans for it in the local press, and distributed copies of a newsletter through the school and the parish council. I only had one negative response – from a taxidermist, of all people – who telephoned to protest about the possibility of 'community' involvement spoiling his private sojourns in the wood. It is the only occasion when I have felt fiercely proprietorial.

Not many local people turned up for the first Sunday working party, and with hindsight I should have spent more time on public relations and not presented the new regime as such a *fait accompli*. But there was a big enough party of my own friends and woodland enthusiasts to tackle what I had rather arbitrarily chosen as the first task, clearing a glade by the pond. We cleared the pond, too, of generations of polythene debris and fallen branches.

As it happened, the thinning of the glade proved to be a more democratic exercise than I had expected. With no real plan other than the vague idea for a clearing which would let sunlight into the pond, we simply sawed away at anything damaged or flimsy on the sunward side. But our volunteers began sticking up for individual trees. A broken oak was pollarded instead of being felled. The hollies (the most aggressive colonizers in the wood) were saved for sentimental and superstitious reasons. I argued for two thorn bushes which a volunteer with forestry training had a predatory eye upon. Finally we ended up with a quite unexpected but communal landscape, not so much a clearing as a glade with groves.

On later working days we carried on this tradition of talking through the fine details of thinning and path-making as we went along. But this became more difficult as the numbers of people turning up to help grew. On fine Sundays as many as 50 people might spend some time working in the wood, and in the areas where trees were actually being felled and reduced to firewood, the activity could become quite frenetic. I am amazed, thinking about those early days, that we escaped without anyone being injured. There seemed to be something almost compulsive about the desire to get to grips with the trees. No sooner had one been felled – and, with luck, missed the reception committee beneath it – than it was stripped of branches, logged and stacked. It rarely took more than a few minutes, and when I paused to watch, it reminded me of those speeded up films of jungle ants reducing a dead animal to a skeleton. I don't entirely understand the roots of this demented energy, but I know that I felt it myself. I don't think it is destructive, but has something to do with the exhilaration of physical contact with trees in the open, with the smell and feel of freshly cut wood, even the sound of the poles clattering on the stacks.

Not that it was all hard labour. Work days became very sociable events, helped usually by a large bonfire. Some older visitors were quite content to spend the day chatting and carrying the odd twig to the fire. But it was the children who had the most sensible attitude to work. They would saw or carry wood furiously for a while, but then suddenly all take off at once, like a flock of birds. A few minutes later we would hear them in the distance, building camps amongst the old man's beard, or swings across the chalk pit. Half an hour later they would all come back to work again.

The big bonfires were one of the many mistakes we made in the early stages. They were part of that obsessive and infections desire to tidy up the natural world that we all had to cure ourselves of. They may have been welcoming but they scorched the earth and wasted tons of wood. Now we just make piles and dead hedges with the brushwood. They rot away in five or six years, and in the meantime make nesting sites for wrens and robins and a habitat for mosses and fungi. We have learned, too, that simply felling a tree does not by itself cause natural seedlings instantly to shoot up in its place. Saplings, like planted trees, need a good deal of light before they begin to prosper. We have even learned to be more patient with the poplars. For a while we regarded them as the wood's bane, a blight on all the native species trying to regain their place, and we felled them remorselessly. But they repeatedly split or snagged up in other trees. Once they were down we hardly knew what to do with them, as they were useless both as firewood and timber. Now we tend simply to hasten their natural decline by ring-barking, and have found that, dead on their feet, they are favourite nest trees for woodpeckers and tits.

We still don't have a comprehensive 'management plan', cut and dried, and I rather hope we never will have. But the wood has begun to respond to our pottering, which is really nothing more sophisticated than a kind of bower building, teasing the wood into patterns of growth that both we – and it – seem to enjoy. Frogs have returned in large numbers to the pond and on mild March days there may be as many as a hundred mating and spawning in the water. You can hear their croaks – one of the first new songs of the year – 50 yards away. The new tracks – not planned on paper, but winding paths cut and trodden out by volunteers just following their feet – are alive with butterflies in summer. Primroses have started to reappear along the tracks, and wherever we have let in more light there has been a surge of wild flowers. In places the wood anemones have become so dense that they can fill the air with musk in April. New generations of young trees – ash, maple and cherry chiefly – have sprung up in the areas we have thinned and are already eight feet tall in places. We have uncovered relics of the past, too: a 90-million-year-old fossil sea urchin that turned up *inside* an old stump, and a sawpit where trunks were cut up before the days of chain-saws.

The economics of the whole operation would make depressing reading for a monetarist. My one purely capitalist enterprise, selling some timber beech thinnings from the plantation, made just about enough profit for us to buy some new saws and put down a deposit on a secondhand pick-up truck. And although we have generated a formidable amount of small wood in the regular 'current account', much of this goes out as free firewood, a reward for anyone who has helped cut it and can carry it away. The remainder we sell locally. Either way it is an exceptionally labour-intensive exercise. Roughly 500 person-hours produces 25 tons of wood, which at current prices means a return of about 50 pence per hour's work.

But none of this takes account of the qualitative economics of the wood, or of mysterious transactions which have more to do with barter, and the peasant principle of buying a stick by cutting it. Moss is gathered by flower arrangers, pea-sticks by gardeners, wood-ash by potters. And people 'buy time' for the wood simply by choosing to spend their leisure there.

Perhaps the most gratifying thing of all has been the return of people to the wood. As the novelty of the working days wore off and fewer volunteers turned up, so the number of walkers and picnickers and woodland hedonists grew. It has been used by botanists, bat-watchers, fungus collectors, even a couple of poachers.

In May an Ascension Day service is held in the wood. The children from the village school tramp half a mile across the fields, come into one of the glades, and surrounded by bluebells and freshly opened beech leaves, sing hymns to new life and crops and the mysteries of transubstantiation. Once, at bluebell time, I chanced upon two lady watercolourists sitting amongst the flowers in immense white hats and looking so utterly at home that I felt like an interloper myself. No one possesses a wood even if they do 'own' it.

*

It has been partly a distaste for playing the squire that has kept my private use of the wood low key. I have had plenty of fantasies about what I might do there. (I have dreamed of an oil-strike, and daydreamed of becoming a ruggedly fit woodcutter.) I resolve each year to spend a whole night there, something which plenty of local children have done. I may even have a piece of furniture made which uses all its native woods. But I doubt if I will ever fulfil my most nagging ambition, which is to go into semi-retreat under the cherry trees, like a scholar-gipsy. I find I can write there when the weather is fine, with my back against a tree in one of the glades, and every spring I fidget with the possibility of building a tree-house, or parking an old travellers' caravan down in the valley and turning it into a writer's den. Perhaps it is just laziness or a fear of vandalism that stops me doing anything about these whims. But somehow they feel too proprietorial, a kind of squatting, and I know that, for me, they would take away some of the surprise, the sense of 'otherness' of the wood.

'Managing' the wood can, ironically, be a narrowing experience, too, although I now have skills I never dreamed of before. I know how to sharpen a chain-saw, cope with the chicken-bone springiness of holly wood, and how fast ash seedlings grow. But work (and perhaps the work ethic) can narrow one's view of nature as much as extend it. Sometimes, trying just to enjoy a stroll round the wood, I find I am trapped in a kind of managerial tunnel vision. I peer obsessively up at the canopy to see if we have let enough light in, scour the ground for regenerating seedlings. It needs a conscious act of will to relax, and remember that life has its own priorities here.

It is worth it. The wood has a wonderfully intricate and seasonal geography. After autumn and winter gales the whole interior is transformed. Drifts of leaves or snow obliterate the paths and leave new trails of open ground between the trees. I walk about as if I have never been in the place before, seeing the other sides of familiar trees. Snow and hoar frost weld the outer branches of the weeping hollies to the ground, forming a kind of protective skirt, and woodcock sometimes shelter on the ground inside. If I get too close they shoot out at the last minute, quite silently, like a stifled gasp, and skim crankily away over the brambles until their chequered plumage merges with the shade.

Just walking in the wood at this time of year shows what a narrow hush separates winter and spring. I scuff the frozen ground absent-mindedly and am momentarily astonished by the mass of white bluebell shoots underneath, poised for their moment. The beech buds, as hard as skewers on the outside, are already full of green tissue. The beech leaves open in late April and early May, but they don't grow gradually, like oak or birch. They unfurl, already full-sized and partly translucent, and can flood a wood within a matter of days. Up at the westernmost corner of the wood, a group of young beeches arch over a track through the bluebells, and most years leaves and flowers open in the same week. With the filtered sunlight dappling the trunks and the bluebells rippling underneath, the whole corner takes on the submerged glow of an aquarium. Up to my knees in flowers I've found myself walking in slow motion here, amazed at the density of the light; and then going back and walking through it all over again.

The pulse of the wood comes through in the smallest corners. These beeches grow on very poor acid soil, and in one shaded patch just a few yards square the vegetation seems to have reached a tacit agreement to share out the meagre resources. There isn't a hint of selfish genes or the struggle for survival. The wood anemones keep to their place, down close to the clay, the wood melick to its, up on the bank. The bluebells never grow more than six inches high, or the wisps of honeysuckle more than a foot. And when the spring growth has died back there is, underneath, a modest carpet of moss. The only sign of change I have seen was when the leaves of a bluebell, normally content with spiking dead beech leaves and carrying them a few inches into the air like brown ruffs, broke through the rotting shell of a fallen branch. Up here this was a major event. This minute oasis of stability won't last, of course; but for the moment it seems like the still centre of the wood, and I love to sit here and imagine the rest of the wood turning more restlessly in the distance.

As for autumn, it often seems like the real beginning of the woodland year. The light begins to seep back, we start work again and the woodland floor blooms once more, this time with toadstools, crushed rowan berries, eddies of blown leaves. There are fairy rings of parasol mushrooms round the holly bushes at the bottom of the wood, and we've sometimes made them into a working picnic, toadstool butties eaten round the fire.

The wood always seems at its best when people are there, especially the children, who seem to have a natural and unselfconscious affinity with trees. I once saw the four-year-old son a friend stretched out, fast asleep, by the side of a wood pile, as straight as one of the logs; and his sister, just a couple of years older, hugging a tree and whispering into the bark.

One afternoon in late February we were cutting a gently curving transverse path about 50 yards long across a compartment in the middle of the wood. We had started work in cold, louring cloud and the threat of a blizzard, but by the afternoon the weather had turned balmy and spring-like, and the sun kept flashing into new corners as the track advanced. Long-tailed tits were prospecting for nests and the first frogs were making their laborious journey back to their pond to spawn. It was hard to concentrate on the work and in the end we all just turned to pottering. Fran and John's children, Alice and Howarth, were trying their hands at flint-knapping, but then noticed the frogs, and spent the next hour tip-toeing up the hill behind them. They had taken it upon themselves to form a frog escort and attended them solicitously all the way back to the pond, clearing the way, and giving them a helping hand from time to time, just in case 'they couldn't get over the branches'.

4

Had it been like this before? There was a not very old tradition of a 'village picnic' in the field next to the wood. Some villagers could remember the time when all the local woods were worked by cross-cut saw teams and the local children would prowl around with shopping bags to gather up wood chips for the home fires. And Fran and John's neighbour once showed us a beautiful basket plaited from hazel and willow by the Italian PoWs who looked after the wood during the war. I found it strangely affecting to think that the men I had stared at when I was a child, marked out by the black diamonds sown on their coats, had been working in Hardings 40 years ago, just as we did now.

Before that, the part played by the wood in the life of the village was obscure, only noted down when important things happened. The Tithe Commutation map of 1841 shows the wood (and most of the surrounding countryside) with the same outlines as today, except that what is now the beech plantation was then a field. The wood was owned by a local woodman called John Garrett. He leased the tiny strip of land which joins the wood to the lane to a small-holder, Mr Burch. (On the map its name is given sardonically as 'Hundred Acres'.)

On the earliest map I have been able to find, dated 1766, Hardings Wood is part of a much bigger tract of woodland, a mile and a half long and a mile wide at its broadest point, which stretched from Wigginton almost to the boundary of Berkhamsted. This, in turn, joined on to the considerable area of commonland shared by Tring and Wigginton, which Henry Guy, Secretary of the Treasury, attempted to convert into a park at the end of the seventeenth century. Defoe described the reaction to this little adventure in his *Tour Through the Whole Island of Great Britain*: 'Mr Guy presuming upon his power, set up his pales, and took in a large parcel of open land, called Wigginton-Common; the cottagers and farmers opposed it . . . but finding he went on with his work . . . they rose upon him, pulled down his banks, and forced up his pales . . . and this they did several times, till he was obliged to desist.'

Before that things are murky. But at some stage the cryptic earthwork known as Grim's Ditch or Grim's Dyke was dug through the wood. It passes through Hundred Acres, along the dry valley at the bottom of the wood and through the lower part of the village, then travels in a moderately straight line three more miles to the south-west. No one is entirely sure what purpose the Ditch was meant to serve, or even when it was created. Trenches and embankments with the same name straggle all the way through the Chilterns. A shallow version cuts across Berkhamsted Common (and is used as a hazard by the golfers). There are fragmentary sections running through the Hampdens, and a much longer reach near Nuffield, which at Nettlebed turns into what is known as the Highmoor Trench. They mostly consist of a simple ditch and slightly raised bank, but the different sections vary hugely in breadth and depth, and may not all date from the same period. The features common to all the sections are that they run either parallel to the western ridge of the Chilterns or at right angles to it, and when they change direction they do so angularly rather than in a curve. They look as if they may have once formed large and roughly rectangular enclosures, and the most plausible explanation is that they were a kind of ranch boundary. But that is speculation and for want of any convincing evidence the Ditch acts like a psychologist's ink-blot test, confirming people in their favourite historical fantasies. At school, where anything remotely straight could only be a Roman remain, we were taught that it was a military barricade, planned by the legions. Some local historians favour an Anglo-Saxon date and have suggested that it was another of King Offa's defensive boundaries. But fragments of pottery from a much earlier date have been unearthed in a section of the Ditch a few hundred yards from my wood, and there are those who suspect it was the work of the Celts, perhaps the Catuvellauni, who inhabited parts of the Chilterns just before the birth of Christ and were known to be great earth diggers and cattle raisers. Whatever the Ditch's origins there is an even chance it was made by slave labour.

The mystery that absorbed me was not this ancient one, but a more recent gap in the records. Some time between 1750 and 1850 Wigginton parish was transformed by a massive programme of 'improvement'. On the 1766 map the parish is shown as almost completely covered by commonland and wood. By the early years of the nineteenth century two-thirds of the woodland has vanished, leaving just five little island copses (of which Hardings is one) amongst the new fields. There is no record of exactly why this clearance happened, but it was presumably the work of the Lords of the Manor, the Harcourts. They were certainly an ambitious family. Some years later, in 1852-3, they petitioned for the enclosure of Wigginton's 300 acres of common. The records of the whole process of enclosure, down to the cheque stubs for legal fees and the surveyor's sketch-maps all survive in the County Record Office.

Most revealing are the minutes of the meetings held between the 24 local landowners and the surveyor during the early months of 1853. They got together in the Royal Hotel in Tring, about a dozen of them at a time, and systematically replanned the home country of 629 people. It was an apt venue. The Royal was a commercial inn, some way beyond the village and next to Tring's new railway station, and was convenient for agents and absentee owners. Here, over lunch, they argued about how much of the common each of them should be allotted and set down the reasons for enclosure: 'increased productiveness of the land, useful employment of labour . . . and improvement in the morals and habits of the people'. And on 7th August, they agreed their plan for reorganizing the parish's communication system. Two weeks later posters went up all over the village, printed in heavy block type, like 'Wanted' notices. Thirteen existing ways and footpaths were to be completely closed and replaced by two surveyor's roads leading to the nearby towns. One of the footpaths closed off was a track leading from the village of Wigginton to the valley, which passed through Hardings Wood. Not the slightest evidence that it ever existed remains.

By the end of the 1853 the enclosure was complete. The fences had been raised and the commoners and landless poor of Wigginton had been left with a two-acre recreation field and five acres of allotment. This miserly gesture was about the norm for this period of Parliamentary Enclosure, but it is still odd that local people did not put up any resistance (as they had two centuries previously). Wigginton had the reputation of being an anarchic parish, and in 1854 a new curate, the Reverend George Gaisford, was appointed to restore order. His private notes about the village – 'a *terra incognita* in the neighbourhood' – in those years after enclosure (regarded as confidential until recently, for fear of offending village sensibilities) provide some revealing comments on the effects of the changes: 'All the picturesque appearance of the place was gone, and perhaps the poetry. Post and rail fences were right and left all over the place. But I believed that the change would morally tend to the benefit of the people: they would be less rough, wild and uncivilised. I cannot judge whether this has happened; whether as some predicted "wicked Wigginton would become virtuous Wigginton". I cannot say that the people as I knew them deserved the former epithet, or differed very much from other people of whom I have experience. But as I look back I am much surprised that they accepted the enclosure as patiently as they did, considering of how many rights the enclosure deprived them.'

*

In 1983 we presumed to do some landscape reshaping ourselves. We badly needed a track to get a vehicle into Hardings to carry cut wood out. We knew we would need a professional contractor to do the final excavation, as it would involve creating a cutting up one side of the valley, but we did most of the preparatory work outselves. We surveyed several possible routes, chose the one with the shallowest gradient, got our felling license and cleared the few trees that lay along the track. The whole site measured no more than a hundred yards long by four yards wide. Then, in early October, we held a 'plant fostering day'. Numbers of local children and their parents turned up, dug up the ferns and primroses that lay along the path of the proposed track, put them in pots and took them home for the winter.

Two days later the Hymac 890 came into the wood. It was a huge yellow machine, normally used for digging agricultural drainage systems, and armed with caterpillar tracks and a prehensile scoop. It's driver, Len, was a shy Londoner who used to make clock cases in Bethnal Green, and he seemed able to use it like a precision instrument. He could nudge trees over, then swoop to catch them before they fell. He could excavate scoopfuls of clay and tuck them underneath the machine to raise his working platform. And all the while he was adding a subtle S-shape to the rather

168

crudely straight route we'd marked out. I became fascinated by the machine, and took to watching it from a perch
higher up in the wood. It shuffled back and forth behind
the trees, purring gently and with only the words 'Agricultural Improvers', appearing whenever it passed into the
open, to mark it out as a foreign force. In my fevered diary
entries for those days, Len and his familiar had already
been gathered into the company of honorary forest
creatures: 'When he is dragging soil back to level out the
track he pulls it back and under himself, as badgers do
when dragging bedding out of their setts . . . all the while
the machine is being followed by small bands of robins, like
tiny gulls after a woodland plough'.

The end product was remarkable – a sinuous, unsurfaced
road lying right in line with the autumn evening sun. Even
after one week its hard edges were beginning to mellow into
a moist, cheesy ribbon of clay and crushed chalk, crimped
at the edges. The first frost and rainstorms brought down
drifts of debris over its bare surfaces – bluebell bulbs, moss,
minature landslides of flint. Within a month there was a
green film of algae over the chalk. In the spring we put the
fostered plants back, and one year later the bank was bristling with young birch seedlings, old man's beard, musk
mallow and wild raspberries. The best new plant seemed
like a nod of approval by the wood. Along the track that
summer after the digging sprung up tufts of wood vetch, a
straggling climber that carries bunches of exquisite lilac-
striped pea-flowers sometimes six feet up into the low
branches. Wood vetch isn't common in Britain, and though
it does occur in the Chilterns it was supposedly extinct in
Hertfordshire. I had certainly not noticed it flowering in
the wood before. In its natural habitat it haunts cliffs and
rocky wood edges, and I like to think that dormant seeds or
small plants, kept from flowering by the shade, had found
the flinty, sun-lit bank of our new track just like home.

But it would be wrong to claim too much credit for what
has become of the track. Although it has made walking
round the wood easier for everyone, our small experiment

in 'improvement' was, like the enclosure of the parish, a private imposition on ancient public territory. Human hands haven't had much to do with the mellowing of the end results into a landscape in either case.

As for Wigginton Common there are a scattering of damp, heathery patches to remind us of what it must have been like before it was fenced off and ploughed out of existence in 1853. But there is barely an echo of that act of corporate vandalism in the landscape itself – just, sometimes, a slight feeling of over-orderliness, of a loss of breathing space in the geometry of the fields. Mostly the landscape seems to be making a continual gesture of reparation. What were once the old rail and post fences are now hedges covered by wild roses, and along the straight enclosure road the verges are thick with self-sown oak trees. Even Grim's Ditch, despite its murky history, always carries the first flowers of spring, a glimmer of celandine and moschatel on the dark banks. Yet this generous flooding back of life has happened in spite of those events in the past, not because of them. It is a mark of real healing, not a kind of memorial scar tissue. All we create are the frameworks for landscape; what fills them, gives them life and texture – the switchback contours of the hills, the tides of flint, the young ashes crowding into gaps where beeches have fallen, the wood vetches climbing into their branches – is, thank goodness, something still beyond our control.

5

The great storms of the late eighties seemed, in some eyes, to confirm the belief that nature couldn't be trusted to look after its own. The October 1987 hurricane, probably the greatest storm for 300 years, caused devastation across southern England and blew over an estimated 15 million trees. The slightly less powerful gales of January 1990 were different in that they came after the leaves had fallen and caused less tree damage as a result. But they were spread over a much greater area. They hit the Chilterns hard and blew over 30 trees in Hardings Wood.

Though much had happened since the 1987 storm, and many of the responses to it been shown up as hasty and wrong-headed, when the wind came again it seemed that nothing had been learned. Within hours we were told that we had another tree disaster on our hands, that the landscape had been irreparably damaged, and – the contradiction didn't seem to be noticed – that the only response was massive repair and 'restoration', by which was meant clearing fallen wood and planting young trees in the gaps. One of the national organizations that sponsors tree-planting reached new heights of sophistry when it stated that 'trees are at great danger from nature'.

The outcry had seemed just as odd in 1987. The morning after the storm I raced up to Hardings Wood with an odd mixture of excitement and foreboding, and was rather disappointed to find that only a handful of birch and poplars had been blown down. The most extraordinary sight in the wood was not the state of the trees, but of the undergrowth. The brambles, strewn with shredded ash foliage, were standing on end, as if they had been backcombed or electrocuted. It was hard to believe the apocalyptic stories which were coming from further south and east, and the following day, Francesca (who also had a professional interest, as gardening correspondent of *The Times*) and I took a long journey into what sounded like the battle zone of the Sussex and Kentish Weald.

Signs of the damage began almost imperceptibly, the way snow cover does when you travel north: at first a few limbs and the odd roadside beech down; then sudden tongues of flattened trees at the edges of woods. Windsor Forest had been badly hit, yet the ancient squat oaks in the Great Park had escaped with the loss of just a few branches. It was Fran, getting her weather eye in, who noticed that they were old pollards whose tops had been blown off during some previous gale, and had been safe this time because of their low centres of gravity.

At first sight the storm seemed to have struck quite randomly, taking hardwoods and conifers, venerable giants and leggy saplings alike. In some of the worst hit areas in north-east Sussex every other tree seemed to be down. We edged the car along by-roads carpeted with frayed green leaves, dodging lianas of fallen power lines and telephone cables that were only inches from the car windows. Already the lanes were lined with sawn trunks and tilting boles, and beyond the thickets, marooned householders were still trying to cut their way out. Some trees had split open all the way along their trunks, and the air was full of that warm, sawmill aroma of resin and raw wood.

It was the patchiness of the damage that was the oddest feature. We would drive through a mile or two of country where the leaves had not even been scorched by the wind, then pass a zone of intense devastation, and see woods with their perimeters intact but centres torn out. Frequently we heard local people attempting to account for this by saying that the wind had 'swooped down', and it is almost certain that there were swarms of tornadoes up in the front of the hurricane, just as there had been in the Great Storm of 1703 (and the forgotten Scottish hurricane of 1968).

But a pattern did start to appear. Shallow-rooted beeches on damp or thin soils were the most vulnerable, especially where they had been deliberately (and often ineptly) planted. We saw one plantation of 20-year-old beeches blown clean out of the ground, and their root-balls were only marginally less cramped than they must have been when they left the nursery. In all species, 100-year-olds (young middle-age for a tree) growing in the open were the worst affected, presumably because they had reached maximum crown volume, and therefore greatest wind resistance, but not maximum root extension. Softwoods like pines and spruce, of course, were often just snapped off a few feet above the ground.

Least affected were very old trees with relatively few remaining branches, and the forestry Jeremiahs who were blaming the 'geriatric, over-mature' condition of the nation's woods for the damage were clearly having trouble thinking beyond their usual frame of reference. Even where the local damage was severe, there was no sense in which 'the landscapes of southern England had been irrevocably changed' – the phrase used by some commentators immediately after the storm. The woods, even where they had lost more than half their timber, were still indisputably woods. The dense Wealden hedges were thin and ragged but still followed the same boundaries as before.

It was understandable that public reaction was one of shock. Familiar local landscapes and favourite individual trees had been transformed. For days after the storms I saw adults and children standing silently around the fallen planes in London squares and parks, looking bemused and grief-stricken. At Kew there was even talk of holding a memorial service 'for the fallen'. Trees were meant to be the bedrocks of the natural world, reassuring landmarks that could be relied on in times of instability and materialism. Now they had been reduced to so much lumber themselves. The vigils over the fallen parish monuments that October marked a reawakening of our latent affection for trees.

Sadly, however, any communal understanding we might have once had about the life of trees was not reawakened at the same time. There was barely even a memory of the role that fallen trees had played in most people's childhoods, when they were important meeting places, hideouts and climbing frames, and lasted with all their fantastic array of burr, knots and rot-holes for decades. Nor was there much acknowledgement that much of what we admired as 'character' in ancient trees – the snarled tops of Sherwood's old oaks, for example – was the result of past storm damage.

Instead the hunger for some kind of explanation and response gave an unprecedented boost to that stubborn, anthropocentric image of the tree as artefact. During the months that followed the full-blown myth was given plenty of airings. Trees, it goes (or at least *proper* trees), can only be grown by man. Woods, parks, hedges, indeed whole landscapes, have been planned and planted by man. If they are damaged by nature, it follows that this is an affront to human skills, an assault (the persistent comparisons with the Blitz helped foster this frame of mind) and must be met by redoubled efforts at planning and planting. At times the storm seemed to be conceived of as an almost animistically malign force. A National Trust catalogue for an exhibition of storm damage paintings declared that 'The great storm desecrated the past and betrayed the future'. The Tree Council predicted that unless 'funds are made available and positive encouragement given to owners to restore these [ancient] woods . . . they will revert to scrub and never recover.' It was an extreme formulation of the view of trees as, in Oliver Rackham's graphic phrase, 'gateposts with leaves'. If they fall down they have to be deliberately replaced. I never cease to wonder how the holders of such views imagine trees – spontaneously and unassisted – were once able to cover most of Britain (and still would, given half a chance: look at any common or railway embankment). Perhaps they believe in another, earlier Fall in the landscape, after which trees could never grow freely again. The outcome of this was a rush to gather funds, clear and tidy up woods, and plant, plant and plant again – often regardless of the condition of the site or the suitability of the tree species. Villages became prey to cowboy chain-saw gangs and opportunist nurserymen peddling quick solutions and runtish saplings. There was opportunism at higher levels, too, with political and civic pressure for fast, publicity-catching action.

Of course, there were many sites – gardens, landscaped parks, towns and streets, strictly commercial plantations – where careful replanting was essential.. But the frantic, ill-considered action in woods and the open countryside during that winter of 1987-88 did more damage than the storm itself. In many parts of the south-east I saw bulldozers crushing young trees, scraping away topsoil that was full of seedlings to 'prepare the ground for planting'.

Yet, alongside this, hurricane storytelling flourished and revealed a rather different attitude towards the storm. I heard from Ronald Blythe of a Day of Judgement scene in his local churchyard in East Anglia, where the yews had all been blown out of the ground, showing the glint of white human bones beneath. Round Selborne they were talking with awe of the 50 or so beeches that had blocked a lane below a hanging wood and had to be shifted by dynamite, which blew the surface of the road to pieces too. And from South London I heard of a group of neighbours who made a heroic expedition at the height of the storm to lash down a rocking street tree with guy ropes. There was a good deal of ambivalence about the storm in most of the stories, and a much greater respect for the resilience of both trees and humans than was being shown by some of the authorities out in the field.

I have to say that I was feeling less and less ambivalent myself. Although the damage to life and property had been dreadful, the more I looked at the effect of the storm on the treescape the more it seemed, in the literal sense of the words, a wonderful and remarkable event. In many places it has blown a breath of fresh air through some of the stuffy, over-managed, landscapes of southern England. I spent half that autumn struggling my way round storm-struck woods, amazed at the patterns of twisting and shearing, at trees which had been turned upside down, at astonishing aged survivors amongst acres of toppled matchwood. Some of the interior landscapes of woods were quite fantastic: vast rootplates of chalk, like minature cliffs, and ponds inside the root holes; green branches split off and speared deep into the ground.

These were just one of the new woodland features that were quite likely to spring back into life the following spring, in unpredictable ways. There were many more. Many of the prostrate trees were quite obviously neither dead nor going to die. They had fallen, full of sap, into damp ground with part of their root systems still connected, and would sprout again from their reclining postures. Providentially, it had also been a magnificent autumn for acorns, beech mast and all tree seeds, and there was likely to be a massive regeneration of natural seedlings as well.

A few weeks after the 1987 storm there was a forecast of another big blow and I thought there might be a chance to actually see a big tree coming down. I went out with a safety helmet, a camera and a chain-saw, sat in a field well clear of an exposed wood on the scarp, and waited. Two hours later I crept home in a soft and balmy breeze, feeling foolish and starting to worry about myself. When a few weeks later I came chokily out of John Boorman's ecstatic film *Hope and Glory* about his childhood in London during the Blitz, I wondered for a terrible moment if I was becoming a hurricane junkie, and if the storm was making up for the wartime childhood I had not quite had.

But there were now plenty of other people making a more optimistic view of what had, after all, been an entirely natural event. And George Peterken's so-called 'catastrophe theory' at last came into its own. George, the Nature Conservancy Council's woodland expert, had been arguing for years (usually to deaf ears) that landscape gardeners' and early ecologists' belief in a natural, settled 'climax' woodland had only prospered because of a temporary bubble of calm weather and philosophical arrogance.

By the next summer the woodland that hadn't been fussed and tidied up bloomed with wild flowers and young trees in a way that hadn't been seen in most people's lifetimes. I walked a beat, every three months, along the most devastated part of the beech hangers at Noar Hill in Hampshire, and have never seen woodland growth like it in this country. There were diagonal trees, decapitated trees, branchless trees, extraordinary split and frayed trees, but very few dead trees. Fallen oaks had simply turned into horizontal trees and were sprouting like newly planted hedges (they reminded me of the fable, quoted in Gabriel García Márquez' *One Hundred Years of Solitude*, of the sailing ship beached in the jungle, its masts breaking into leaf). Trees whose branches had been stripped of foliage were growing intricate twigs, like coral. Bare ash trunks

were swaddled in green epicormic muffs. Some of the
shallow-rooted beech had succumbed, but their root-plates
had hanging gardens of shrubs and flowers. There were air-
borne orchids and pits like Aladdin's caves full of sub-
terranean blossom, sometimes even deadly nightshade
sprung from long-buried seed. And the new generation of
seedling ash, maple and hazel, as dense as grass in places,
was shooting up clean through the wreckage and had put on
three feet of growth in a single season. It was not tidy, or
'well managed' but it was triumphantly alive.

At the National Trust's woods at Toys Hill in Kent, perhaps the most comprehensively devastated site in the
south-east, the ground was covered with seedling birch,
whitebeam, beech and yew. The National Trust workers,
rather more optimistic and imaginative than their catalogue
writers, had sawn off some of the beech trunks, and pushed
the stumps back in their holes, where many of them had
promptly struck root. One of them had also done a piece of
chain-saw sculpture on a forked log and placed it like a fertility symbol standing out over the new views of the Seve-
noaks weald. It was splendidly rude, but seemed to catch an
echo of the ancient iconography of the Tree of Life, which
has always been as much about hope for the future as the
rootedness of the past.

6

It is late May again, and baking hot. Perhaps we are in the
greenhouse already. I have been walking about the combes
at the far end of the ridgeway, and everywhere the spring
growth has been astonishing. Last month in Hardings
Wood, I surprised a pure white fallow buck and his hind
lying under an oak tree. They galloped off through the
bluebells and vanished among the beeches. The Norman's
deer had crossed the valley at last, after nearly 700 years!

Yet as old barriers in the landscape dissolve, new ones
form. I have come to the site of a local waterworks, a chalky

enclave that has long been a famous local wild flower site. I used to come here searching for fly orchids. Now it has been privatized, and I fear for its future. All the gaps in the fence have been boarded up, so I must go the back way round to get in, along the middle of a dark double hedge, over the fallen beeches in the scarp woods that rise above these few acres of buffer land. Not far off I can hear the low bark of a guard dog, the new territorial song of a countryside whose freedom is draining away by the day.

But, just for today, the landscape is winning. Ash and birch and willow trees are colonizing the abandoned chalk pits, improvizing a landscape that would horrify a planner, but which is what, left alone, will creep back up the hill to heal the shattered hanging woods. The foliage is dappled and airy, and in the light shade there are spotted orchids, with flowers as sharply sculptured as porcelain, growing between the feathery brushes of horsetail, a combination no gardener could better. There are chiffchaffs everywhere. They are the woodland bird of the year, nesting in Hardings for the first time and relishing the undergrowth in all the storm-struck woods I have visited. I sit on a bank and listen to them just as I did when I was a teenager. High overhead there are small bands of swifts on afternoon expeditions, flying perhaps out of the colonies that still thrive in the school and parish church. Many will be on their third year of continuous flying since leaving the nest, an incomprehensible two million miles ago.

What is it that makes us so moved by the signs and territorial movements of other species? Are we being reminded of our own animal ancestry, of maps and calendars encoded deep in our biological make-up? Are creatures like mediums, passing messages to us about the world? The American writer Lewis Thomas has written of the earth as a single cell, and has imagined 'the whole organism . . . singing to itself . . . Global hormones, keeping balance and symmetry in the operation of various interrelated parts, informing tissues in the vegetation of the Alps about the state of eels in the Sargasso Sea, by long interminable relays of interconnected messages between all kinds of other creatures.' Perhaps humans are the imagination of the planet. I can no longer hear swifts, but watching them now I can feel the stream of their flight, and anticipate the exact moment when the tide-race of wings will burst into a spray of individual birds. I feel as if I am responding not just to them but *through* them, that they are part of what links me to this place, this day, this moment of the year. They seem just as the Field did, like a second skin, prickly with sensation and meaning, inseparable, yet living its own life beyond me.

References

p.8 Fraser Harrison, *The Living Landscape*, London, 1986

p.9 William Hazlitt, 'A Farewell to Essay Writing', 1828

p.15 Metroland, Metropolitan Railway Company, 1932

p.16 Graham Greene, *A Sort of Life*, London, 1971

p.39 Vera Barclay, *Joc, Colette and the Birds*, London, 1934

p.42 William Hazlitt, 'On the Love of the Country', 1814

p.44 Richard Jefferies, *The Story of my Heart*, 1883

p.74 John Berger, *A Fortunate Man*, London, 1967

p.85 Oliver Rackham, *Trees and Woodland in the British Landscape*, London, 1976; *Ancient Woodland*, London, 1980

p.87 Fleur Adcock, *Selected Poems*, Oxford, 1983

p.94 *The Journals of Gilbert White*, ed. by Francesca Greenoak, London, 1986-89

p.99 Geoffrey Household, *Rogue Male*, London, 1939

p.130 Barry Lopez, *Arctic Dreams*, New York and London, 1986

p.144 H. J. Massingham, *Chiltern Country*, London, 1940

p.149 Humphrey Repton, *Observations on the Theory and Practice of Landscape Gardening*, 1803

p.150 Lord Eversley, *Commons, Forests and Footpaths*, 1910

p.165 Daniel Defoe, *A Tour through the Whole Island of Great Britain*, 1724-6

p.176 Gabriel García Márquez, *One Hundred Years of Solitude*, London, 1970

p.178 Lewis Thomas, *The Lives of a Cell*, New York, 1974

Acknowledgements

My warmest thanks to the many people I've discussed parts of this book with, and who have helped clarify many of the ideas and made up for my lapses of memory, especially my family: Edna, Pat, David and Gillian Mabey. Also: Nigel Ashby, Ronald Blythe, Sue Clifford, Jeff Cloves, David Cobham, Janet Cobham, Alan Cummins, Miranda Cummins, Jean Davis, Tony Evans, Liz Forster, Vivien Green, Francesca Greenoak, Howarth Greenoak, Rachel Hamilton, Robin Hamilton, all helpers in Hardings Wood, Tara Heinemann, the staff of the Hertfordshire County Record Office, Anne Kelleher, Alice Kilpatrick, John Kilpatrick, Angela King, Anne Mallinson, Edwin Mullins, Peter Newmark, George Peterken, Oliver Rackham, Elizabeth Roy and Colin Ward.

To Robin McIntosh for her diligent work and calm organization during the preparation of the manuscript. To Annie Norton for her sensitive work on the text, and to my editor, Sarah Wallace, for her unflagging faith in the book and patient good humour in waiting for its protracted arrival. Finally, to Richard Simon, whose two decades of indomitable walking, all-weather friendship and wise counsel have found many echoes in this book.

Some parts of the chapter entitled 'Away Games' first appeared in a different form in the *Independent*, the *Telegraph Magazine*, and the *Sunday Times Magazine*. My thanks to the editors of those publications.

The author and publishers gratefully acknowledge permission to quote from 'Proposal for a Survey' by Fleur Adcock taken from her *Selected Poems* (1983), published by Oxford University Press.

Index

Index

Index

Index

Index